THE CO PARENT

THE CO PARENT

The Toolkit for Parenting Together, Apart

AARON DALE

GREEN TREE
LONDON • OXFORD • NEW YORK • NEW DELHI • SYDNEY

GREEN TREE
Bloomsbury Publishing Plc
50 Bedford Square, London, WC1B 3DP, UK
Bloomsbury Publishing Ireland Limited,
29 Earlsfort Terrace, Dublin 2, D02 AY28, Ireland

First published in Great Britain 2026

A catalogue record for this book is available from the British Library

Library of Congress Cataloguing-in-Publication data has been applied for

ISBN: TPB: 978-1-3994-2757-9; ePUB: 978-1-3994-2756-2

2 4 6 8 10 9 7 5 3 1

Typeset in Aestetico by Lumina Datamatics Ltd
Printed and bound in Great Britain by Clays Ltd, Elcograf S.p.A.

FSC www.fsc.org MIX Paper | Supporting responsible forestry FSC® C018072

To find out more about our authors and books visit www.bloomsbury.com and sign up for our newsletters

For product safety related questions contact productsafety@bloomsbury.com

I never imagined I would be writing a book, so sitting here writing a dedication feels very unfamiliar. Part of me feels uncomfortable doing this, but maybe that's exactly why I need to start here.

I want to dedicate this book to myself. Aaron, this is a reminder of what's possible. A reminder of what you're capable of. A reflection of everything you've had to overcome to get here. This is for the boy who carried a weight he didn't understand how to put down. The boy who longed for a connection with his father that never came. The boy who grew up without a clear example of what love between parents looked like. The boy who spent 30 years figuring life out and another 10 questioning himself.

This is also for every child raised in a single-parent household, whatever that looked like, or still looks like, for you. For every parent carrying the load alone, feeling uncertain, overwhelmed and stretched thin. You are not crazy for thinking the way you do. You are not wrong for wanting the other parent to show up in the way your child deserves.

I dedicate this to Nan, who is no longer here. You were never able to meet my sons or witness this moment, but I know, without you, none of this would have been possible.

And to Mumsy, for showing me what resilience truly looks like, and for always holding space for me, even now at this big age. This book is yours just as much as it is mine.

Contents

Introduction

Before we begin, I want to thank you for purchasing this book and immediately let you know that you are not alone. Whether co-parenting is something you've been navigating for a while or you're just starting out, I want to emphasise that you are not alone. No matter how stressful your current situation may or may not be, or how unique you feel your circumstances are, I promise you there are millions of men and women experiencing the same thing. You are stronger than you think and I guarantee that more of this is in your control than you might believe.

Go on social media and you will come across countless videos discussing parenting and co-parenting as though there is one easy-to-apply formula, yet anyone who's lived it knows it's rarely that simple. You see, no matter what you watch or read online, co-parenting is never one-size-fits-all.

I wrote this book because I saw a gap. There are plenty of resources about parenting and relationships, but not enough that speak directly – but more importantly, practically – to the realities of co-parenting, especially when it's complicated, inconsistent or painful. You and your co-parent are two unique individuals raising another unique individual. Along the way you'll experience a wide range of emotions, personalities and challenges, and that's completely normal.

This book is your co-parenting toolkit. As you move through these pages, you may find that some sections don't apply to your current situation, but that's okay. Over time, different parts will resonate in new ways, offering a gentle reminder that you're not alone; reassurance when things feel uncertain; advice just when you need it most; and guidance to help you stay grounded and child-focused, because when we lead from a place of care and clarity, rather than ego, spite or resentment, we create the most nurturing space possible for our children and for ourselves.

Whether you're managing a functional arrangement, navigating tension and conflict, or doing it alone because the other parent is largely absent, you deserve support, coherence and connection, because when you feel supported and confident, your child – and whenever I say 'child', if you have more than one then I also of course mean 'children' – benefits from the calm, stability and love that flows from you.

Regardless of where you are in your co-parenting journey, the one thing that remains constant is your love for your child. That love is the foundation. No matter how difficult things are between you and your co-parent, you must always return to that base. The truth is, while your relationship may have ended, the responsibility of raising your child together never does. This book will not only remind you of this, but will also help you navigate the process. It is for:

- Parents who are committed to putting their child first, even if the co-parenting relationship isn't easy or doesn't exist at all
- Co-parents who get along 'well enough', but who want to improve their communication and consistency
- Parents who are struggling with an uncooperative, distant or emotionally charged co-parenting relationship
- Single parents who are doing it alone due to an absent or unreliable co-parent, who want to understand how to navigate that, for themselves and their child.

The seed for this book was planted and grown as a result of years of real experience, trial and error, honest reflection and conversations with other parents trying to do their best by their children, even when circumstances are far from ideal. Your child didn't ask to be part of the break-up and they shouldn't have to bear the weight of any unresolved conflict, so my goal is to help you to concentrate on them and their well-being.

Every co-parenting relationship starts from a different place, but whether your separation was amicable or filled with heartache, there's always a path to creating a healthier environment for your child. My hope is that by sharing my insights, you will be empowered to create a space where your child feels loved, supported and secure, no matter what happened between you and your ex-partner.

Whether you're figuring out how to communicate better, set boundaries, avoid resentment or simply raise a happy child in a complex situation, this book will provide you with insights and tools – with something real, useful and reassuring. In the chapters ahead you'll find advice on setting boundaries, maintaining healthy communication, managing finances, dealing with new relationships, navigating special occasions, blending families, and much more. You'll also find actionable strategies and ideas to help you navigate the complicated world of co-parenting, while always keeping your child's best interests at the fore. Having said that, this book can't possibly cover every single angle and aspect of co-parenting, but I have featured the main themes that come up time and time again in my work.

About me

My name is Aaron Dale and over the past 17 years I've experienced the highs and lows of co-parenting with two children – my sons Omari and Tyler – from different relationships. I've learned many hard-won lessons and I'm here to share them in the hope that your journey will be smoother than mine was.

At the end of 2021 I decided to open up and share a small part of my life on a friend's podcast (thank you, Jamie!). To my surprise, the response was incredible and people connected deeply with my honesty, especially when I spoke about co-parenting. That's when I realised how important this conversation really was.

For a long time, co-parenting had felt like a taboo subject. I remember starting a new job and being asked by colleagues if I had children, as happens when you're getting to know each other. I'd say yes, but I'd stop short of mentioning that I wasn't with their mother. There was a sense of hesitation, maybe even embarrassment, particularly being surrounded by older colleagues who seemed to have the 'traditional' family set-up. But over time, I came to understand that every family looks different, and that's okay.

Even families who stay together don't always find happiness. I wanted to change the narrative and normalise conversations around co-parenting, and made it my mission to be open, honest and vulnerable, to comfort, guide and inspire anyone who might be on a similar journey, even if at the time that was just my 900 followers.

Fast-forward three years and that small community had grown to nearly a million followers across all platforms, which is proof of how many people are craving real, honest conversations about co-parenting. In that time I've hosted live shows featuring open discussions with panels of men and women, appeared on BBC Radio, collaborated with respected brands and connected with celebrities I've long admired, yet I truly believe this is only the beginning. *The Co-Parent* marks the next step in that journey – a deeper, more personal way for me to reach and help even more people who are navigating the world of co-parenting.

However, my understanding of co-parenting isn't just from my experience as a father; it's also shaped by my experience as a son. Raised by a single mother with a largely inconsistent father, I know at first hand what it's like to be caught in the middle. I've seen how a failure to co-parent disrupts a child's sense of stability and self-worth. That's why I'm passionate about this topic – because I've lived it from both sides.

When my first relationship ended at 22, I thought I had life figured out. How wrong I was. I didn't understand manhood, let alone fatherhood. My examples of what a father was came from TV shows like *My Wife and Kids* and *Everybody Loves Raymond*. I desperately wanted to be the kind of father I saw on those shows. I failed to realise that to build a family like they had, I needed to understand what a healthy relationship looked like; something I had never seen in real life. The only relationship I had witnessed growing up was between my mother and an abusive partner, which was far from healthy.

When my eldest child's mother and I parted ways, emotions were raw and communication seemed impossible – mostly because of my ego. I thought that having a child together gave me more power than it did. It took years of her setting boundaries and being consistent with them, alongside me growing and understanding what my role as a father was, before things got easier.

Parenting is one of life's most rewarding yet challenging journeys, because it reveals who we once were while also reflecting who we are now. No matter how little we communicated or how immature our behaviour became, one thing always brought us back to the table: our son. We both wanted what was best for him, even when we couldn't agree on much else. One of the first lessons I learned was that co-parenting isn't about fixing your relationship with your ex – it's about building a new partnership with them for the sole purpose of raising your child.

Through my platform, @Raisingboys2men, I've connected with thousands of parents all over the world who are trying to navigate this process. I've seen how common the struggles are and how deeply people crave practical guidance. This book is about understanding that shift and making that mindset change.

Before we begin

Before we go any further, I need to make something clear: this book will NOT change your co-parent. It will not magically transform them into the person you hoped they would be and it will not hand you the 'perfect' co-parenting partnership.

People often ask me what caused the shift – how I became the co-parent I am today compared to the man I was at the start of this journey. The truth is simple: I saw the negative impact my own actions were having on my child, and I made a choice: I wanted better for him. Love is not just a word or a feeling; love is an action. And I do not believe we can truly say we love our children if our behaviour and choices tell a different story.

Thankfully, as I got older, I met some great examples of men I was able to learn from, people like my barber Vinton and my colleague Maurice, whom I met in one of my first full-time jobs and who went on to become like a big brother to me. But, ultimately, the change came from one place: my desire to give my child something better than I had experienced growing up.

Change is not comfortable. Change is not easy. I had to shed a lot of skin to become the man I am today. I had to face my childhood, my father's absence, my mother's journey, my relationships and my friendships. I had to understand why certain things trigger me and have honest, vulnerable conversations with the people around me.

None of that was comfortable, but all of it was necessary.

What often happens is that we excuse the need to change. We find reasons to justify our behaviour and create barriers that prevent us from taking accountability or making amends.

There may be moments throughout this book that make you reflect, and that reflection may feel uncomfortable. In fact, you may have been given this book by someone else and felt resistant before even opening it. You may find yourself thinking about times when you allowed your ego to lead you. Times when you blocked contact, withheld financial support, spoke badly about the other parent, used your child as a weapon, or caused harm to your child through your actions and behaviour.

This is not to dismiss anything that has happened to you or any pain you may have experienced. It is simply to say that by opening this book, you have already taken a step in the right direction.

That is a massive win for your child.

Because I genuinely believe it is difficult to read this book, reflect honestly and not become a better version of yourself. And if you become a better version of yourself, there is a very good chance you will become a better parent for your child as a result.

Whether your co-parent is cooperative, inconsistent, difficult or completely absent, my aim is to support YOU to show up in the healthiest way possible for your child and for yourself. You cannot control another person. Not a co-parent, not a friend, not even your own child. No matter how right you believe you are, the only person you truly have power over is yourself. That is what I will bring you back to, again and again:

- Your mindset
- Your choices
- Your actions

The important thing to remember is that children thrive in safe, stable and nurturing environments, and these conditions can be found in any type of family. Throughout this book you'll see the words 'mother' and 'father,' but I want to be clear: families come in many forms. Two mothers. Two fathers. Single parents. Blended families. Extended families stepping in. And everything in between. Wherever you sit in that picture, if you are committed to raising a child with intention, compassion and consistency, this book is for you.

Part One

Co-parenting foundations

#1

What successful co-parenting really means

I don't know what has brought you to this book. Perhaps you're someone who is already co-parenting, perhaps you're considering ending a relationship and transitioning to co-parenting, or perhaps you're expecting a child you'll raise alone.

Whatever your reasons, I know one thing: if you've picked up this book, you care about doing what's best for your child. Caring for your child also means caring, in some capacity, about their other parent. Half of your child comes from this person and that connection is not something to take lightly. This doesn't mean you still love that person, want to be with them or even want to have regular conversations with them. Instead, it means recognising their importance in your child's life.

When we first become parents, we often envision what our family will look like – the dream home with the white picket fence, the Range Rover out front and maybe even a basketball hoop in the garden. I know I did. We create these perfect pictures in our minds of what our family will be and what it will look like when our child is raised in that ideal environment. In the same way, we might also create an image of what the perfect co-parenting relationship should look like. We dream of getting along with our ex, of being able to share family outings together, embracing each other's new partners without resentment, celebrating birthdays together and maybe even offering advice about future relationships to each other.

These ideas are not inherently wrong, but they often come from a place of personal fantasy rather than what's best for your child. It's easy to get lost in the notion of what we *think* co-parenting should look like, forgetting that our primary focus should be on the child and their emotional well-being.

We might look at other co-parents who seem to have it all together – the ones who can go on family outings, attend birthday parties and even be 'friends'. And while that might seem like the picture-perfect co-parenting dynamic, the reality is that there are children in those same families who are unsettled, confused or hurt by the situation. So, if those external markers of success of shared holidays, joint celebrations or friendly interactions aren't the true measures of successful co-parenting, what are?

As parents, you are both vital to your child's growth. One may provide sunlight and the other water, but both are crucial to how the seed grows. However, when the relationship between parents changes, due to infidelity, incompatibility, toxicity or maybe even never having been in a serious relationship, co-parenting can become complicated. No matter why you're no longer together, you're here because you're committed to doing right by your child.

While the research on single parenthood and its impact on children is clearly complex and sometimes contradictory, a growing body of evidence suggests that factors like strong, stable relationships, parental mental health, socioeconomic status and access to resources play a more significant role in a child's success than family structure alone.

I have two sons, and people sometimes ask why I never made it work with either of my children's mothers, as if that decision was solely in my hands. The truth is, I wasn't the man I am now during those relationships and I would never have become him without the journey I've been on.

Growth isn't linear: it requires time, mistakes and lessons learned along the way. Real growth is sitting back and seeing the mother or father of your child happy with someone else, and feeling nothing but joy for them. That's *child-focused co-parenting*. It's understanding that the other person's happiness directly impacts your child's emotional well-being.

Successful co-parenting is measured by one thing: *the well-being of your child*. It's the environment in which your child feels safe, loved and valued, regardless of the status of your relationship with their other parent. You are no longer romantic partners, but you are partners in parenting. And that requires communication, respect and compromise – none of which are easy when emotions run high.

Defining the 'co' in 'co-parent'

Ultimately, you have the power to define what the 'co' in co-parenting stands for. It could represent:

Conflict
When parents fail to see eye to eye it can create an atmosphere of hostility.

Confusion
Inconsistent messaging from parents leads to confusion. Clear boundaries, communication and roles help prevent mixed signals that can destabilise your child's environment.

Contempt
Allowing personal grievances to affect parenting can lead to toxic relationships. By keeping respect at the core of co-parenting you can avoid creating negative emotional baggage for the child.

Or it could, on the other hand, mean:

Communication
Open, honest dialogue is the foundation of successful co-parenting. It's about listening as much as speaking, ensuring that both parents are heard and that the child's needs are always at the centre.

Cooperation
Effective co-parenting requires a shared effort. It's the willingness of both parents to work together despite personal differences, for the common good of raising a happy and healthy child.

Collaboration
Co-parenting is not a competition; it's a collaboration of two homes working together with the best interests of the child at heart.

Consistency
Children thrive in stable and consistent environments. If you are both providing this, it creates a sense of security for your child. Whether it's enforcing rules or maintaining routines, a unified approach reduces confusion for the child.

This book aims to help the 'co' mean something positive, because all children deserve the best, especially those growing up in co-parenting situations, and it's up to us to ensure they get it.

Key terms used in this book

Language around parenting, particularly co-parenting, can carry a lot of emotional weight and often people use terms to reflect their personal circumstances, sometimes even to validate or justify how they feel. That's human, but it's also the reason why discussions about what counts as a 'single parent', who qualifies as a 'co-parent' or what makes someone 'absent' can get heated or confusing.

You've probably seen it online where someone shares their experience, uses a familiar term and suddenly there's a debate in the comments over whether they 'qualify' for that label. So, to avoid confusion and to keep this book focused on solutions and support, not semantics, I want to be clear from the start about what I mean when I use certain terms.

Where possible, I've included formal definitions drawn from dictionary sources or organisations working within the family and parenting space. These aren't the only definitions out there, but they'll shape the conversations we're going to have throughout this book.

Co-parent/co-parenting

The *Oxford English Dictionary*'s definition of a co-parent is: 'A person who shares the duties of bringing up a child, especially when the parents are separated or not in a relationship.' In this book, a co-parent is someone who is no longer romantically involved with the other parent, but who still shares some level of parental responsibility for their child. Co-parenting refers to the ongoing interaction, decisions and responsibilities shared between two separated or divorced parents raising a child in different households, but this book acknowledges that co-parenting looks different for everyone.

Single parent

According to the *Cambridge Dictionary*, a single parent is: 'A person who has a child or children but no partner living with them.' There's an ongoing debate about whether someone can be considered a 'single parent' if they have an involved co-parent, and some argue you're only a single parent if you're doing everything alone – financially, emotionally, and practically. In this book, a single parent means a parent who is not in a romantic relationship or cohabiting with their child's other parent. That includes parents who are actively co-parenting, but live and parent separately, as well as parents whose child's other parent is inconsistent, absent or uninvolved. So yes, you can be a single parent and a co-parent or a single parent with no co-parenting relationship at all.

Primary parent

In this book I do sometimes talk about the primary parent, but I want to stress that when both parents share a true 50/50 care arrangement there is no primary parent in the way people often assume. This is because both parents share time, responsibility and decision-making equally. From their child's perspective, they don't have one 'main' parent – they have two parents who show up equally.

However, you will often find that you can't escape the term 'primary parent', as it may still appear in paperwork or crop up in professional settings. For example, schools, doctors and courts may require a lead contact and address. This is not a reflection of importance, but simply administration, so a healthier way to view 50/50 parenting is that the child has two primary parents.

Absent parent

'A parent who is not involved in their child's life, either physically or emotionally' is how the Oxford Reference website defines an absent parent. That description works for me, but I'd add that having little to no involvement in their child's life could be by choice, through estrangement, due to legal restrictions or because of a complete breakdown in the relationship.

#2

You are not the 'baby mother' or 'baby father'

Let's look a little more closely at language, because the words we use shape the way we see people. They carry weight. They create labels. And sometimes, without meaning to, those labels strip others of their humanity, value and importance.

I'll be honest: as a young man, I used the term 'baby mum' without thinking twice about it. That wasn't because I was trying to be disrespectful, but because it was what I'd heard. On TV. In music. From older men around me. It rolled off the tongue so casually, like a throwaway phrase. But what I didn't realise at the time was this: every time I said 'baby mum' I was unknowingly keeping both the mother of my child and our child stuck in a moment, as if our son would forever be a baby and she would never be anything more than the person who gave birth to him. It ignored growth, erased her ongoing role as a mother, and reduced our journey to a single event instead of a lifelong responsibility.

> That term didn't acknowledge the human being raising my son.
>
> It didn't reflect the love, the effort, the sacrifice.
>
> It didn't hold any of the respect that should come with being someone's co-parent.

And the same goes for 'baby father'. These terms freeze us in time, as if the child we created is forever a baby and the connection between us holds no room for growth, maturity or shared responsibility.

Think about it. When people are married or in relationships, we don't say, 'That's my baby mum'; we say 'my wife', 'my partner', 'my husband'. We focus on the relationship, not just the child. We speak from a place of connection, not convenience, and that should not change after separation.

Because the truth is that person is not your 'baby mum'. They are your son's mother. They are your daughter's father. They are your co-parent, someone you are forever linked to through the most important role either of you will ever have: raising a human being. So before we dive into the rest of this book, I want to ask you to make a shift. A mindset shift. A language shift. A respect shift.

> Replace the label.
>
> Honour the role.
>
> Speak with intention.

Not just for the sake of the other parent, but for the child watching both of you, learning what love, respect and partnership really look like.

> Let's start there.
>
> Let's start better.
>
> Let's move forward not as exes at war, but as co-parents with a purpose and shared goal.

#3

Should I stay or should I go?

It's important to acknowledge that not everyone reading this book will have separated from their child's other parent. You may have spent weeks, months or even years caught in what feels like an emotional hamster wheel, revisiting the same thoughts, feelings and fears over and over again. It's exhausting. And yet one question keeps resurfacing: should I stay or should I go? It's a question so many co-parents have faced at some point and what makes it so hard to answer is the very person you love the most – your child.

In a typical relationship where no child is involved, the decision to stay or go can seem straightforward, with acts such as infidelity or abuse providing you with instant reasons to leave. However, when a child is involved, we often set aside our morals, values, needs and comfort for what appears to be the benefit of the child.

Fears of leaving

Society often tells us that two parents are better than one and this narrative can weigh so heavily on us. We're conditioned to believe that there's no such thing as a perfect relationship, that things could always be worse, and because of this we settle for less than we deserve, fearing what might happen if we step into the unknown.

We can easily become entangled in financial obligations, too, such as shared debt and mortgages. It can feel like an impossible trap and for some of us, age adds another layer of uncertainty. The idea of beginning again when you've invested years into a relationship is frightening and you know that leaving means losing the stability you've fought so hard to maintain, especially for your child.

But let me tell you right now: none of these reasons are worth sacrificing your mental and emotional well-being for – not one of them. Your peace of mind, your happiness and your sense of self are priceless. Leaving a toxic or unfulfilling relationship is not only about choosing yourself, but also about teaching your child what love and happiness truly look like.

A 2019 Sheffield University study looked at the experiences of over 27,800 households with children over a six-year period. It found no evidence of a negative impact on children's well-being from living in a single-parent household. In terms of self-reported life satisfaction, quality of peer relationships and positivity about family life, children from single-parent homes scored just as highly – or even higher – than those from two-parent households. The key takeaway from this study is that what truly matters for a child's well-being wasn't the number of parents under one roof, but the quality of the relationships in that environment.

A word from Daniella Kadene, child psychotherapist

In my work with children, young people and families, I have seen that structural changes in families are an increasingly common experience for young people, and in many cases, everyday disagreements between parents have little lasting impact on children. However, when a parental relationship becomes chronically conflictual, marked by ongoing hostility and emotional instability, the effects on children can be significant.

Research suggests that prolonged exposure to high levels of conflict can place a child's nervous system in a constant state of alert. When this happens, the parts of the brain responsible for survival become overactive, while those involved in thinking, reflecting and emotional regulation become less accessible.

As a result, children may develop an overreactive stress response and show signs such as anxiety, impulsivity, aggression, disturbed sleep, difficulty concentrating, emotional numbness, dissociation and symptoms associated with trauma.

Living in an environment where tension and unpredictability are ongoing can mean that a child feels constantly unsafe. When fear, sadness or confusion arise in relation to the very people who are meant to provide protection and care, this can deeply affect a child's sense of trust and security. Over time, they may develop complex emotional defences as a way of coping with a world that feels unreliable.

When children do not yet have the emotional capacity to understand or express these feelings, distress is often communicated through behaviour. They may act out, withdraw, or struggle in school and relationships, not because they are 'difficult', but because they are overwhelmed. These behaviours are often unconscious attempts to manage intense emotions and to signal a need for support.

Sadly, such behaviours can sometimes lead to negative responses from parents, teachers or other professionals who may not recognise them as expressions of distress. Instead of receiving understanding and care, the child may encounter criticism or punishment, which can reinforce feelings of shame, isolation and misunderstanding.

You can have two parents living together in constant conflict, with a child stuck in the middle, dreading coming home, losing sleep, not eating properly, and feeling torn between their mum and dad. That's not a healthy environment. If your relationship has become toxic, and has been for some time, I urge you to consider whether staying together is better for your child.

If you are feeling low, stressed out, worried, anxious ... guess where that energy is being transferred? To your child. If you are feeling positive, happy, excited, good about yourself ... guess what energy is getting transferred to your child?

Sometimes, separating and creating healthier environments in two homes is far more beneficial than keeping up appearances in one unhappy home. Your child wants to see you happy, but that may not be together – it may be on your own or even one day in a different relationship.

Setting an example

Your child doesn't want to grow up knowing that the reason their mum or dad stayed in an unhappy relationship and suffered was because of them. Imagine the guilt they'd carry later in life, knowing their parent remained in misery for their sake.

And remember, they're learning about relationships by watching yours. They need to see what a healthy relationship looks like; what it means to be respected, valued and cherished.

They learn from watching how you interact with your partner, how you speak to each other, touch each other, and how you manage conflict. They are a sponge, soaking up everything they see from your relationship, good and bad.

Children learn about love, respect and partnership from their parents. If they grow up witnessing tension, sadness or indifference between you and your partner, that will shape their understanding of relationships.

If your child sees you in love, smiling and truly happy, they'll learn what a healthy, fulfilling relationship looks like. It's not just about protecting them from the negatives, it's about showing them the joy and peace that come from being with someone who respects and cherishes you.

Your child will expose the cracks

It's essential to understand that if your relationship is already unstable, adding the complexities of parenting will only make those weaknesses more apparent. And that's not to say you can't work through them, because many couples do, but it's important to go into this journey with clear eyes and realistic expectations.

Every situation is unique, and only you can decide what's best for you and your child. What I do believe, though, is that parents don't need to stay together to raise healthy, well-adjusted children. I like to think that, despite being apart, the mothers of my children and I have done a fantastic job raising our two young kings.

But if I had my way, would I have chosen this path? Absolutely not. No one goes into parenting fantasising about being a single parent. We start with the hope and belief that things will work out, that our love will only grow stronger with the arrival of a child. Some of you might even have had a child hoping it would mend a relationship that was already struggling. You're not alone in thinking that a child could act as the glue to hold everything together, but let me remind you, a child won't fill the cracks in your relationship; they'll make them more visible.

A better way to think about it is to imagine your relationship as the foundations of a house, which have some small cracks – some you can see, some you can't. When a child enters the picture, it's like placing a heavier load on those foundations. The weight of raising a child doesn't hide those cracks; it exposes and deepens them.

Everything that was fragile or strained becomes magnified under the pressure of parenthood. That's because raising a child requires immense emotional bandwidth as well as extreme resilience. Any unresolved tension in the relationship will rise to the surface. The point is that children don't fix relationships – they reveal them.

There's no shame in recognising that a relationship has reached its limit and that separating might create a healthier environment for your child. What matters is how you navigate the parenting journey, together or apart. At the end of the day, parenting is about building a safe, nurturing environment for your child, not about holding on to a broken relationship. Whether you are together or apart, your ability to raise a healthy child depends on the love, respect and cooperation you can show each other.

Relationships have seasons

It's important to understand that relationships, like everything in life, go through seasons. There are summers full of warmth, but also winters where things feel cold and stagnant. It's unrealistic to expect eternal sunshine and just because you face challenges doesn't mean it's time to leave.

Sometimes, we need to appreciate certain moments, give grace and allow people room to grow. None of us are perfect and if you believe that perfection exists it's worth considering that maybe the issue isn't the relationship, but the unrealistic expectation.

So, as you reflect on your journey, remember that it's okay to choose yourself, but it's also okay to choose patience and grace. The most important thing is to make a decision rooted in truth, growth and the well-being of you and your child.

For those of you who have decided to part ways recently, or are thinking of doing so, I understand that this may be pulling heavy on your heart, allowing multiple emotions to run through your mind, most of which are negative. Have you made the right decision? Are you being selfish? Will your child blame you? Are you being a bad parent?

Leaving a relationship can be one of the most painful decisions you ever face and when children are involved, the emotional weight is multiplied. You're not only dealing with your own feelings of hurt, anger and loss, but you also have the responsibility of guiding your child through this transition. It's important to recognise that while leaving a relationship may feel like tearing apart a family, it's sometimes the healthiest choice for everyone involved, including your child.

A word from Daniella Kadene, child psychotherapist

What is often seen is, with consistent emotional safety, supportive relationships, and opportunities to be heard and understood, children are remarkably resilient. While parents are often central to this process, there are times when they may be overwhelmed by their own distress and unable to offer the stability their child needs. In these moments, support from other trusted adults such as therapists, teachers, extended family members, or mentors can be especially important.

When children experience curiosity, compassion and emotional consistency from the adults around them, rather than blame or fear, they can begin to feel secure again. Over time, this sense of safety allows their nervous systems to settle, their emotional worlds to become more manageable and their capacity for trust and connection to grow. With the right support, even children who have experienced significant conflict can move towards healing, confidence and a stronger sense of self.

REFLECTION: RELATIONSHIP STATUS

For those of you in a relationship you are questioning, take a moment to reflect on the following questions. They are not meant to push you towards one decision or another, but to help you look inwards and reflect on your truth.

How do you feel in your relationship on a daily basis?
Are you content, anxious, frustrated or drained? Recognising your day-to-day feelings can highlight whether your relationship is adding value to your life or taking away from your peace of mind.

Do you feel supported and respected by your partner?
Respect and support are foundational to a healthy relationship. If these are lacking, it can begin to ruin your self-esteem and emotional well-being. Is your partner being a positive influence or a source of emotional strain?

If your child were in your shoes as an adult, what would you want for them?
View your relationship from a different perspective. What would you desire for your child's future relationships? And are you modelling a healthy dynamic for them to emulate?

If your child turned 18 and moved out tomorrow, would you still want to be with this person?
Separate your role as a parent from your relationship with your partner. Consider whether you're staying for the child's sake or

if there's still genuine love and connection between you and your partner.

Has your love for this person changed? If so, why?
Love can evolve and sometimes it fades. Explore how your feelings have shifted over time. Are your reasons for staying rooted in love or simply in comfort, fear or obligation?

Without mentioning the child, what was it about your relationship with this person that you love the most?
Look beyond your role as a parent and focus solely on the connection between you and your partner. By identifying what you cherish most about the relationship, you will gain insight into whether those qualities still exist, have faded or were perhaps never truly fulfilling. This can help you separate the love you feel for the person from the responsibilities you share as co-parents, offering clarity on whether the relationship is still worth nurturing.

If you take only one thing from this book, let it be this: every tough phase, every bad relationship, every difficult moment you've ever faced, you got through it. Your track record of surviving hard times is 100%. You, my friend, are undefeated. So regardless of what decision you choose to make, be it today or in the future, remember that you will be fine.

#4

Why leaving isn't quitting

Leaving a relationship, especially one where you've invested so much time and energy, can feel like starting over from scratch, but it's not just about healing from the break-up. It's also about rediscovering and rebuilding your sense of self. I want to guide you through those difficult moments, offering support and clarity as you work to protect your peace, your child's well-being, and your ability to move forward with strength and intention.

Know that depression lingers in the past and anxiety stems from worrying about the future. The past is behind you – it cannot be changed – and while the future remains uncertain, the choices you make today are within your power. The present is all we truly have control over and this is where your focus needs to remain. Focusing on the present moment allows you to let go of the weight of past pain and release the grip of future fears.

Staying in the now is crucial for healing and rebuilding. Use this moment to prioritise your well-being, nurture your relationship with your child, and create a foundation for a fulfilling life.

Deciding to go it alone

Making the decision to leave a relationship, especially one where a child is involved, does not mean you've failed. It's not quitting. It's not letting your child down. And it's certainly not placing them at a disadvantage, no matter what the 'stats' or outside voices might suggest. The truth is, so many parents don't make the choice you're about to make or perhaps have just made, but that's not because they're stronger. It's because it's hard, heavy and complicated.

A 2019 study by Direct Line revealed that, on average, parents stay in relationships over five years longer than they would if they didn't have children together. That's 7.6 million parents holding on – not because they're happy, but because they believe it's the only option. Of these, 4.5 million said the decision to stay was mutual, but for 3.1 million it was a silent struggle – one they kept to themselves.

And here's the part most people don't talk about: 38% of those children knew. Whether they were told directly (18%) or picked up on it themselves (20%), they could feel the shift. Kids are far more intuitive than we give them credit for. They know when something's off. They can hear the tension, feel the silence and sense the disconnect.

Even among those parents who stayed, the reasons varied – and they weren't always noble:

- 46% of men said they stayed because they believed having both parents in the home was best.
- 31% of women said they stayed because they couldn't afford to leave.
- 23% of parents feared the impact of separating while their children were still young.
- 20% stayed because they needed help raising their children.
- And another 20% because they simply couldn't afford to separate.

I share these stats with you not to overwhelm you, but to remind you that you are not alone in what you're feeling. It may be tough, it may be lonely, but it is not rare.

Imagine what those children witnessed over five years in a home where love had left the room. The unspoken tension. The arguments they overheard. The affection that was missing, even the eye contact that was often avoided, along with the forced smiles.

Now imagine something different. A home filled with peace. A parent who is present, not just physically, but emotionally and mentally, too. A child who sees what it means to choose peace over comfort, acceptance over avoidance.

The decision to leave is never taken lightly.

But it's a powerful decision that says, 'I choose to start healing over constantly hiding.'

This is not failing. This is what courage looks like.

Avoid the blame game

At this point, you may find yourself in one of two spaces. Perhaps the decision to separate was mutual, like the 4.5 million parents who sat down and agreed that it was time. Or maybe you're among the 3.1 million who held it all inside, wrestling with your thoughts in silence until something gave way.

You might be the one who ended the relationship or you might be the one who didn't see it coming. Whichever path led you here, know this: the most important part of your story starts now. Not with blame, not with reliving the break-up, but with the choices you both make from this moment forward.

Because what matters now, more than how the intimate relationship ended, is how you begin your relationship as co-parents. Not just for each other, but for your child. They didn't ask for this, but they are watching, and how you both carry yourselves from this point on will shape how safe, seen and supported they feel in this next chapter of their life.

You have not failed

Over the years, I've spoken to thousands of co-parents and one common thread in so many of their stories is the feeling of failure. It's heartbreaking, but it's real: the feeling that, because we didn't stay together as a couple, somehow we've failed both ourselves and, most painfully, our child.

That idea of failure often comes from a place of guilt. Maybe we feel we've failed our child by not providing them with the family we once imagined, or perhaps we feel we've failed by not holding on to a relationship that society told us we should.

When you take your own emotions and stack them on top of the constant narratives displayed across social media about the 'downsides' of co-parenting and single parenthood, it becomes far too easy to feel overwhelmed, even to feel like you've somehow failed. But let me be absolutely clear: we have to stop defining 'successful parenting' as two people staying in a relationship and raising a child under the same roof.

I have a good friend who is a chef. I was speaking to them the other day, admiring their recent reels, and said, 'All the food you post makes me so hungry.' However, their response completely shocked me. They replied, 'Half of the time it's not even edible.' To which I said, 'Huh? What do you mean?'

They explained that to create that perfect video they often have to record the same steps over and over again. How the sunlight might disappear halfway through shooting, so they have to continue the next day. They even admitted that certain foods are deliberately undercooked because it makes them look better on camera.

By the time they capture that final, flawless image the food is stone cold – beautiful to look at, but nothing you would ever actually eat. And that's exactly how relationships and family dynamics can be. From the outside, the picture might look impressive – matching outfits, big smiles, coordinated posts and 'perfect family' energy – but the reality can be undercooked, cold or carefully edited to hide the parts no one wants you to see.

What happens when we zoom in on that 'perfect family'? What happens when we see what the photos don't capture, what the smiles are hiding and what the carefully curated moments are covering up? Success isn't in the appearance; it's in the reality you create for your child. And if you're showing up with love, intention and consistency, even across separate households, you're already doing far more than many 'picture-perfect' households will ever do.

There are thousands of couples who stay together out of convenience, fear or comfort, not out of love or strength. Some do this without children, but when a child is added to that environment, the pressure intensifies, the cracks widen and the stakes become higher.

And yet for many of us, this child, this amazing individual we created, becomes the very reason we find strength we didn't know we had.

The strength to say 'no' to what's not serving us.

The strength to remove ourselves from unhealthy situations.

The strength to build boundaries that protect our well-being and, more importantly, the well-being of our children.

That strength does not come from failure. It comes from growth, from self-love and from the deep, unwavering love you have for your child. There are people who will criticise you and question how leaving the other parent shows love to your child, but in your heart you know it does and I want to convince you of that fact, too.

Sometimes the bravest thing you can do as a parent is walk away.

Sometimes the most powerful way to express your love to your child is to separate from the other parent.

Sometimes the greatest gift you can give your child is the version of you that refuses to settle for anything other than the best.

Here's the truth: you will never have cause to regret prioritising the version of you that chooses peace, that chooses healing and that models what self-respect truly looks like.

Your child won't remember the relationship you didn't stay in.

They will remember the love you consistently showed.

That is the real legacy.

#5

Don't compete with your co-parent

Although parenthood is a significant part of your life and a very important role, it's important to remember that this role doesn't define who you are. You're still Lily, Mike, Louise, Maurice – whoever you were before the moment you became a parent. Your identity doesn't vanish and yet, for so many of you, it does.

Your friendships, your hobbies, the things that make you who you are, remain just as important, maybe even more so now than ever before. These activities or interests of yours are what help to keep you grounded and fulfilled, and when you nurture those parts of yourself, you bring your best self to the role of being a parent.

By taking care of yourself, you're also caring for your child, because a better you is of direct benefit to them. And with this in mind, it's just as vital to wish the same for your co-parent. Why would you want the person who's equally responsible for raising your children to be unhappy, lost or struggling? A co-parent who feels fulfilled is a better parent, which ultimately benefits your child.

There's often an unspoken sense of competition between co-parents, as if one has to be the better parent – almost like there isn't enough room for both to be genuinely happy, supported and appreciated.

I have a friend who barely gets a moment to breathe. She's raising two children on her own, balancing school runs, bedtimes, dinners, bills, travel and everything in between. It was clear to me that the weight of it all was starting to take its toll. What she needed wasn't just a break; she needed space to recover mentally, emotionally and physically. I said to her, 'Why don't you book a holiday and ask their dad to have the kids for a few days?' Her answer: 'He'd never agree to have them if he knew I was going away.' Meanwhile, he takes breaks whenever he wants, no questions asked.

It made me think, how often do we forget that the person raising our child needs to be in the best possible space to do so? Parenting isn't a competition, it's a shared responsibility. Imagine stepping on to a plane knowing your pilot had only had a few hours of sleep all week and they were tired, stressed and running on empty. Would you still feel safe flying with them? The same principle applies here. When we fail to recognise when the other parent needs rest, it's not just them who suffers; your child does too.

Putting safe parenting first

Did you know that the same pilot flying you to your holiday destination has had to do a self-assessment beforehand? This is called the 'IMSAFE' checklist. IMSAFE (I am safe) is an acronym to help pilots assess their physical and mental fitness before a flight. The letters stand for illness, medication, stress, alcohol, fatigue and emotion/eating. Now what if we replace 'pilot' with 'co-parent' and 'aircraft' with 'child' to check that we as parents are okay? Now the acronym would stand for something like this:

I for illness

Does the parent have any current or recent illness that could affect their ability to care for their child safely and patiently?

M for medication

Is the parent taking any medication that might influence their mood, energy or ability to respond to their child's needs?

S for stress
Is the parent under any stress that might impact their patience, focus or emotional presence with their child?

A for alcohol
Has the parent consumed alcohol recently and could it affect their judgement, alertness or ability to care for their child responsibly?

F for fatigue
Is the parent feeling tired or sleep-deprived, and have they had enough rest to engage and respond effectively to their child?

E for emotion/eating
How is the parent feeling emotionally? Have they had enough to eat and drink, ensuring they're physically prepared to care for their child?

If a pilot ever feels unfit to fly, they must communicate it immediately and another pilot steps in to take control. Why? Because the safety of everyone on board depends on it. Co-parenting should work the same way. It's not just about sticking to your 'scheduled hours', it's about making sure that whoever is caring for your child is in the right mental and physical state to do so.

When one parent recognises they're not in that space, whether due to stress, exhaustion or personal challenges, the other parent should be willing and ready to step in. Not as a favour, but as a shared responsibility to ensure two things:

1. The child remains safe, loved and cared for.
2. The parent who needs time can rest, recover and return to their role as the best version of themselves.

Co-parenting is never about keeping score. It is about finding a healthy balance that works for everyone involved, not just one of you.

When to reach out

I understand that some of you are walking this journey alone, with no support, with no help and sometimes with no contact at all with the other parent. There's no one to tag in when things feel overwhelming and no one to share the load during the difficult moments.

That's why it's so important to regularly check in with yourself and recognise when you need support. This might come from friends, family, your wider community or professional services.

Asking for help is never a sign of weakness. It's a sign of a caring parent who understands that their child's well-being is directly connected to their own. A parent who knows that for their child to be okay, they have to be okay, too.

#6

Letting go of your anger

The hurt you feel is real. The anger you may have towards the other parent is valid, but for you to move forward along this co-parenting journey, you will need to let go of the past.

This doesn't mean pretending nothing ever happened or that you weren't wronged. It's not about dismissing the things that were said or done that caused you pain. Letting go simply means saying to yourself, 'My love for my child is greater than my dislike of the other parent.'

This won't happen overnight. It may take months, maybe even years, of working through these emotions, but it is possible if you remain focused on what matters most – your child.

The anger you hold on to has the potential to turn into energy and that energy can seep into your child's world, creating tension and confusion. Even though it's difficult, the responsibility falls on you to protect your child from the emotional fallout.

Instead of allowing the hurt to linger, shift your focus to the future, because that's the only thing you can control. What's done is in the past. It's a chapter in your story, but it doesn't determine how the story ends.

Live in the present

As I've said, depression stems from dwelling on the past and what has already happened, while anxiety arises from worrying about the future and what may or may not come to pass. However, it is only in the present moment that we are truly alive and capable of making an impact, and to heal you'll need to focus your attention on this very moment, to ensure you prioritise you and your child's well-being above any lingering resentment.

What I'm about to ask may sound impossible, but you can get to this place and, when you do, it will be so freeing for you and incredibly beneficial for your child. This place can't be bought, it can't be faked and there are no shortcuts to getting there. It takes time, maturity and a deep focus on your child. But it is possible. I'm talking about reaching a point where you truly wish the other parent happiness, even after all the pain, and in time you will be able to say – and truly mean – the following:

'I wish you happiness in your new life. I always want to see you shine, because you are the other half in this parenting journey we accepted together. Your joy is joy for our child and your peace is their peace. As we walk separate paths we are grateful for the gift we've been given. I let go of where we've been, I'm thankful for where we are and I look forward to where we are going. We are still a family, still parents, still blessed.'

This might seem impossible now, but reaching this point is about freeing yourself from the weight of the past. It's about finding peace in knowing that the relationship may have ended, but the parenting journey continues. It's about teaching your child what grace, love and maturity look like, even when things didn't turn out the way you hoped.

Resetting the algorithm

Here is a concept that helped me better understand the power of my actions and the patterns I was unconsciously feeding, especially when it came to relationships and co-parenting.

You see, on social media we all have a 'For you' page or similar – a feature within an app that serves us content it thinks we'll be interested in. However, that content doesn't show up by accident. It's based on what we watch, engage with, save, share and revisit. In short, the app pays attention to your habits. ▸

If you consistently watch toxic debates, drama or negativity, the app says, 'You must like this' and keeps feeding you more of the same. On the other hand, if you're watching videos about healing, growth or parenthood, guess what? You start seeing more of that. The app doesn't judge; it simply reflects your behaviour back to you.

Life works the same way. There's an algorithm at play – not digital, but deeply human. What you focus on, engage with emotionally, give your energy to and repeat begins to shape what shows up in your life. If you constantly dwell on betrayal, bitterness or blame, life begins to feel full of it. If you're stuck in toxic patterns, chasing validation, repeating unhealthy dynamics or engaging in destructive arguments with your co-parent, don't be surprised if those same patterns keep showing up, just with different faces or situations.

Some people say, 'Why do I keep attracting the same type of person?' or 'Why is my co-parenting relationship always full of conflict?' But maybe the harder truth is that it's not just what you're attracting, it's what you're interacting with. It's what you're feeding, consciously or unconsciously. Just like the app, life is saying, 'Oh, you keep responding to this? Here's more of it.'

The good news is you can reset the algorithm. It starts with small decisions – choosing to walk away instead of arguing; choosing to respond, not to react; choosing peace over proving a point; choosing growth over comfort. In a toxic co-parenting dynamic, that might mean letting go of needing to control what your ex does or learning how to disengage from patterns of conflict that no longer serve your child's well-being.

The more you practise healthy boundaries, intentional parenting, self-respect and emotional discipline, the more life reflects that back to you. Slowly but surely, your 'For you' page starts to look different – not because the world changed, but because you did.

#7

Let's talk about statistics

In the UK, around 42% of marriages end in divorce and many of these families move into co-parenting arrangements. In fact, over 2.5 million separated families are currently raising children together across the country. This means that about one in three children grow up in a household where parents are co-parenting, often across two homes. In the US, the trend is similar, with 40% of children experiencing life with parents who are no longer together and nearly 16 million parents actively co-parenting. In the 21st century, co-parenting is becoming not just an arrangement, but an integral part of how families function.

When we actually look into the stats around single parents, it paints a very different image than the one society has created for us, with characteristics such as being young, unemployed and uneducated, yet the data shows otherwise.

The average age of a single parent is between 37–39-years old and less than 1% of them are teenagers.

More than half (55%) have only one child and almost half (44%) have previously been married.

In 2022, Dame Rachel de Souza, the Children's Commissioner for England, published a report highlighting the different types of family settings, including single-parent households, blended families and co-parenting arrangements, in which children are now growing up. This shift, while often viewed with concern, brings important opportunities to rethink what family means, and how we can best support children's emotional and developmental needs in a modern context. Crucially, De Souza emphasised the importance of emotional security, parental involvement and communication over traditional markers of family, and this is backed up by studies that have repeatedly shown that children thrive in environments where they feel secure, loved and supported, regardless of the family structure,

Rather than mourning the decline of the traditional family, we should open the door to celebrating new, diverse family models and focusing on the positive outcomes they can produce, especially when parents prioritise the well-being of their children. What's key is that the success of these modern family models does not depend on whether parents are together, but on the love, care and support the children receive.

So, the good news is that co-parenting, when handled with care and cooperation, can be immensely rewarding. Research shows that children raised in cooperative co-parenting environments are more likely to feel secure and supported as they grow, despite the changes in family structure. For separated families, this should be a source of hope and motivation. The focus must be on the quality of parenting, not the structure. The decline of the 'traditional family' does not signal the breakdown of family life – it signals the evolution of what family can be – and co-parents who communicate effectively, cooperate in decision-making and maintain a loving connection with their child can offer the same, if not more, emotional security and stability as a two-parent household.

Challenging the stigma

Since starting the @Raisingboys2men platform I have come across countless pages, articles and podcast clips about the negative effects of single parenthood. There's certainly a persistent narrative around single-parent households that paints them as inherently flawed environments where children are destined for failure, but as a man who was raised in this 'flawed' environment, and someone whose children are being raised in it, too, it's important for me to debunk these myths.

Single parents are often raising children who are just as likely to succeed as those from two-parent families. For example, according to data from Gingerbread, the UK charity that supports single parents, over

70% of single parents in the UK are in work, challenging the outdated stereotype of the unemployed single parent and demonstrating single parents' dedication to providing for their child, even while managing the demands of sole parenting. Despite the challenges single parents often face, such as financial pressures and balancing work with childcare, Gingerbread paints a picture of resilience and strength – values that single parents are likely passing on to their children.

Of course, for every stat you come across that supports an opinion or rhetoric, there will probably be one that contradicts it, so it's up to you what you choose to allow to fill the space in your mind, but suggesting that children from single-parent homes start life at a disadvantage compared to their peers from two-parent families is wrong and harmful, because the stigma doesn't just affect the parents – it also casts a shadow over the children, framing them as 'less than' before they've even had a chance to define their own lives.

Single parents are fathers, too

There are so many misconceptions about co-parenting and one of the most common is that all single-parent households are headed by women. While single mothers do make up the majority, it is important to recognise the substantial presence of single fathers, too. Many assume single parenthood is an experience exclusive to women, which can lead to an underappreciation of the challenges and contributions of single fathers. This perception can marginalise them, limiting the support and resources available to them.

In the UK, the proportion of single parents who are fathers has remained around 10% for over 15 years and currently stands at 12%. In the US, data from the 2024 census revealed that there are around 7.75 million single parents raising children under the age of 18. Of those, around 1.6 million – or one in five – are single fathers.

While single mothers still make up the majority, these figures highlight a significant and growing number of single-parent households led by fathers, demonstrating that single fatherhood is not an anomaly, but a reality that deserves recognition and support.

Academic performance

It's another common belief that children raised in single-parent households are destined to underperform academically compared to their peers from two-parent families. This assumption suggests that the absence of one parent inherently disadvantages a child's educational journey and, as a single parent, this type of narrative may fill you with guilt, apprehension and worry about the educational hurdles your child may face, the opportunities they may miss out on and their long-term success.

However, contrary to this belief, there is research indicating that parental involvement plays a more crucial role in a child's academic success than family structure. Parental involvement in children's early education is consistently found to be positively associated with their academic performance and research published in the Journal of Educational Psychology found that parental involvement, parental expectations and the quality of parental support were significant predictors of children's academic achievement. The findings suggest that the quality of parental engagement plays a crucial role in educational outcomes.

A word from Andrez Harriott, founder and CEO of The Liminality Group

In one of my podcast episodes I had the privilege of speaking to Andrez Harriott, whose work is all about shifting the futures of children most at risk of falling into criminal behaviour or already caught up in the system. (You might also know Andrez from the iconic – and one of my favourite R&B groups – Damage.)

Andrez broke down a critical truth: adverse childhood experiences (ACEs) – those deeply impactful events like neglect, abuse or exposure to violence – don't discriminate based on family structure. ACEs can happen in single-parent homes, ▸

two-parent households or even within families that look perfect from the outside.

Substance misuse, domestic violence, financial instability, bereavement and even extreme cases like homicide are issues that transcend race, class and family set-up. These challenges don't care whether you're working class or living in a mansion in Mayfair. They exist everywhere. The difference lies in how these experiences are managed or ignored.

When trauma becomes a daily occurrence, what experts call 'complex trauma', it compounds, leaving deep emotional, mental and physical scars. Complex trauma doesn't just pass with time; it shapes how a child views themself and the world, often carrying into adulthood. What really puts children at risk isn't being raised by one parent or two – it's growing up in an environment where adverse experiences are constant and unresolved.

Changing the narrative

A child raised by one parent who is present, attentive and loving can thrive just as much, if not more, than a child in a home filled with conflict and neglect, and we have to rethink the way we approach this conversation.

The narrative about single-parent homes needs to evolve. It's time to stop blaming the family set-up and start addressing the real issues. It's time to challenge the outdated belief that single-parent households are synonymous with struggle and disadvantage.

The outdated idea that single-parent households are inherently problematic totally misses the mark. The focus shouldn't be on the structure of the household, but on whether the home is a safe, stable and nurturing space for children. Love, support and consistency are the building blocks of healthy development, rather than the presence of two parents under one roof.

#8

The other person's perspective

Along this co-parenting journey you and the other parent will both walk completely different paths while raising your child, each experience shaped by unique challenges, even if you share a 50/50 split.

Though you may both love your child deeply and want what's best for them, the way you navigate your roles as parents may differ greatly. There will be moments when emotions run high, when communication feels difficult or when you may not feel comfortable enough to express how you really feel. This is the reality for many co-parents and it can be isolating, so I've created a space within this book to share the raw, unfiltered experiences of others, with the hope that it will enable you both to understand and reflect.

For some, there are days when the weight of parenthood feels unbearable and articulating that weight can seem impossible. Whether you're the primary parent or the non-resident parent, there are moments when it feels like you're carrying the world on your shoulders. These emotions are valid, and acknowledging them can be the first step towards understanding the struggles that come with co-parenting.

Over the years I've had the privilege of hearing many single parents share their experiences on my social media platform. It's been eye-opening and humbling to learn from others who are walking similar paths, and it inspired me to take action. I asked a question that I felt would resonate deeply with many: 'What is your biggest struggle as a co-parent?' The responses flooded in, each one unique, yet many with similar themes. As I read through them I realised how important it is to hear from both sides: the primary parent and the non-resident parent.

In this chapter I am sharing those struggles, so that we can build a sense of understanding and connection. Knowing that others are facing similar challenges can give you comfort and strength, and my hope is that you'll feel heard and validated, and that your co-parent will gain a deeper insight into what you may be facing as you raise a child together.

The primary parent

For many primary parents, the daily grind of being the sole caregiver can often feel like an overwhelming weight. The responsibility of ensuring that your child's needs are met physically, emotionally and mentally often falls squarely on your shoulders. But it's not just the tasks at hand; it's also the emotional labour involved, sometimes without the support of a partner.

I've heard from many primary parents about the exhaustion that comes from being the main decision-maker, provider and the person who handles the child's daily needs. One parent shared, 'I carry the mental load of everything. If I don't do it, it doesn't get done. There's no one to share the responsibility with on a day-to-day basis and it's emotionally draining.'

The primary parent is often the one who feels like they're constantly in the trenches. Whether it's the financial pressures of bringing up a child on a single income, or the emotional toll of being the one to set boundaries and maintain consistency, it can feel like an endless battle. But even with all these challenges, most primary parents show up for their child, often with little acknowledgment or relief.

If you are a primary parent, please feel seen. You deserve to feel supported, heard and understood. Your struggles are real and your emotional labour is valid. You may feel like you're doing everything on your own, but the sacrifices you make do not go unnoticed as your child is always watching.

The non-resident parent

A different set of challenges is faced by the non-resident parent. Although they may not carry the day-to-day responsibilities as heavily as the primary parent, the struggles they face are no less valid. From the emotional toll of not being the constant presence in their child's life to the feeling of being disconnected from the daily routine, the non-resident parent is often navigating a difficult path, too.

One non-resident parent shared, 'I feel like I'm missing out on so much of my child's life. I only get snippets of their day-to-day and it makes me feel like I'm not part of their world.' Another described a common struggle: 'It's so hard to make decisions about my child when I don't have a say in everything. I feel like I'm on the outside, trying to stay involved, but often feeling powerless.'

Despite their best efforts, non-resident parents may feel disconnected from the decisions that shape their child's life. The lack of influence over everyday choices can lead to feelings of frustration and helplessness. Additionally, seeing their child less frequently, especially if they are dealing with a difficult co-parent relationship, can create a sense of guilt and anxiety.

It's important to recognise the struggles of the non-resident parent, too – you want to be present, you want to help, but the barriers often feel insurmountable. It's easy to overlook your challenges when you aren't physically there every day, but your mental and emotional load also deserves attention. Your desire to remain connected, to do right by your child and to support your co-parent is often just as strong, even if it looks different.

The power of understanding

I hope that by sharing these experiences from both sides, primary and non-resident parents, you can begin to appreciate the complexities of the co-parenting journey. It's not easy for anyone involved and there will always be moments of struggle. But as we reflect on these shared experiences, it's important to remember that the goal is not to compare or blame, but to connect, understand and support one another. The more we can acknowledge the difficulties each side faces, the better we can navigate this challenging journey together.

Whether you're a primary or non-resident parent reading this, I hope the words resonate with you and remind you that your struggles are not unique. I hope this also gives you a deeper understanding of what your co-parent may be experiencing. And, above all, I hope both sides can find compassion for each other and work towards creating a co-parenting relationship that puts the well-being of your child at the forefront.

REFLECTION: SEE IT THROUGH YOUR CO-PARENT'S EYES

Empathy is like a cooling gel. It soothes tension and restores connection, especially in co-parenting relationships. It's not about excusing poor behaviour, but about acknowledging the challenges your co-parent faces and using that understanding to bridge the gap for the sake of your child.

In moments of frustration or misunderstanding, pause before reacting. Take a breath, step back and try to see the situation through their eyes. The following points will guide you:

- **Step into their shoes:** Consider the daily challenges they face that may not be visible to you.
- **Acknowledge their feelings:** How might guilt, frustration or disconnection influence their actions?
- **Pause before judging:** What pressures could be shaping their choices?
- **Appreciate their effort:** How do they show love and commitment, even quietly?
- **Reflect on communication:** How can you listen more openly or express yourself with empathy, keeping their struggles in mind?

By using these points you give yourself space to pause and consider rather than react. That pause alone can prevent unnecessary conflict, diffuse situations before they escalate ▶

and help you respond with empathy for what the other parent may be experiencing.

Our ego often wants to be right. It pushes us to be louder, firmer and more direct, but in co-parenting being right rarely moves things forward. Understanding does. When you choose empathy over ego, you move closer to the shared goal that matters most: creating a calmer, healthier environment for your child.

#9

The co-parent triangle

When a child is born in a heterosexual context, three relationships are immediately formed:

1. Mother and child
2. Father and child
3. Mother and father

Together, these three connections form a triangle. At the top of that triangle is the child. At the base are the two parents, mum and dad – or mother and mother, or father and father, depending on what form your family structure takes.

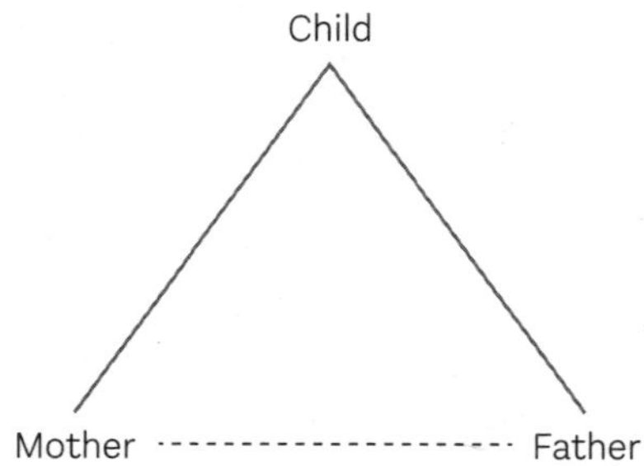

The child sits at the top for a reason. They are the priority and they should be the focus. Everything is built to support and raise the child. The child is held up by both parents, even if those parents are no longer together. The triangle's strength comes from each parent supporting the child independently *and* being able to cooperate at the base when necessary.

Now let's talk about the base: the parents. In the diagram opposite, the reason why this line is visually different is because the relationship between these two people can take various forms. These two adults may be in a loving relationship. They may be married. They may have had a brief connection. They may be divorced, separated or never had a healthy relationship to begin with. And sometimes, they may even actively dislike or avoid each other.

But here's the truth many people miss:

> The nature of their personal relationship with each other does not change the fact that each of them is still a parent to the child.

Their emotional dynamic, whether warm, cold or hostile, has nothing to do with their individual responsibilities to the child, because each parent has two distinct roles in this structure:

1. The personal relationship with the other parent.
2. The individual parenting relationship with the child.

These roles must never be confused. What often causes conflict in co-parenting situations is when one co-parent mistakenly believes that:

> Because they are no longer with the other parent, their parenting role and responsibility has somehow reduced or become less important.

But that's simply not true. It's a common mistake – too many people, mothers and fathers alike, start withdrawing from their child's life once the romantic relationship ends, but the truth is:

> The line between parent and child should nearly always remain intact, even if the line between the parents is broken.

Your connection to the other parent may fade, shift or end entirely, but your connection to your child is for life. It is not conditional. It doesn't depend on your relationship status. It doesn't depend on how you feel about your ex. And it certainly doesn't vanish because things became difficult.

Co-parenting begins when romance ends

The moment the romantic relationship ends, a new relationship begins – the co-parenting relationship. However, the relationship between you and your child remains the same, even if you and your co-parent no longer speak very often. In fact:

> You may not see eye to eye.
>
> You may not even like each other.
>
> But the child you created normally still needs both of you to show up.

So, no, you don't need to be best friends and you don't need to agree on everything, but you do need to honour the shared responsibility you have as parents, because children shouldn't carry the weight of broken relationships. Instead, they should be lifted up by two people who may no longer be together, but are still committed to raising them together.

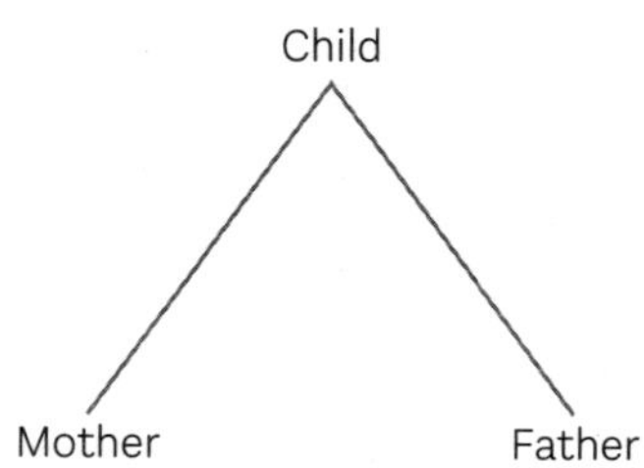

The child is still at the top of the triangle, with the parents supporting them, but as you can see in this version of the triangle, there is no line connecting the mother and the father. No friendship. No romance. No communication and yet they are still in place, holding up their child.

This is a powerful reminder: you don't have to be connected as a couple to be connected by purpose. The structure of the triangle remains solid as long as each parent stands firm in their role. When one parent steps back, disappears or refuses to carry their share, the triangle becomes unbalanced. One side is forced to overcompensate, to stretch, to bend, to carry the emotional, physical and financial weight that was always meant to be shared.

And over time, that strain shows up in the child. In their confidence, in their sense of safety, and in their understanding of love, trust and what it means to be supported. Your child should never have to suffer because the adults could not work together. Even if there's no love left between the parents, there must still be commitment to the child you both brought into this world. So, ask yourself:

- Am I holding up my side of the triangle?
- Am I showing up as a parent, regardless of how I feel about my co-parent?
- Am I willing to rise above resentment, silence or ego for the sake of my child?

Because at the end of the day, it's not about your past relationship.

It's about your present responsibility.

The line between you may be broken, but your child still deserves to be held up by two parents, not one.

#10

Parenting versus co-parenting

When I say the word 'co-parent' to you, chances are your mind immediately creates a picture of your ex-partner. You think of that individual, perhaps your relationship with them, maybe even how they treat your child or how they've treated you in the past. But what happens when I say the word 'parent'? Instantly, your focus shifts to your child. You think of your responsibilities towards them, the bond you share and the importance of your role in their life.

There is no 'I' in parent, but there is in co-parenting. The moment you become a co-parent, it's easy to make it about you, not about your child, but your role hasn't changed. Your focus must remain on them, not on what you're entitled to and not on your personal needs.

If we pause for a moment and shift our focus, we'll see that parenting and co-parenting are not two different jobs. They are the same job with one key difference: the structure of the adult relationship has changed. But they are two sides of the same coin, and what doesn't change is the child's needs.

What is parenting?

At its core, parenting is the act of raising a child from infancy to adulthood. It's about guiding them through each stage of their growth – physically, emotionally, socially and intellectually. Parenting is far more than providing food, shelter and basic care. It's about:

1. Keeping the child safe and healthy.
2. Preparing them for life as independent adults.
3. Teaching them values that reflect the family's culture and beliefs.

These are the core responsibilities of parenting, but it goes deeper than that. Every decision you make, every action you take, helps shape your child's character, sense of responsibility, motivation and sense of self.

In fact, parenting is more about actions than words. Children learn far more from what we do than from what we say. Leading by example is one of the most powerful tools we have as parents. Whether it's through family outings, playing together or just spending quality time with them, these shared moments help prepare your child for life and strengthen the bond between you.

Above all, parenting is about love. It is what holds everything together, especially in difficult times. When your relationship with your child is rooted in unconditional love, it becomes the glue that keeps you connected to your child through disagreements, misunderstandings and challenges. A hug, a shared laugh, or even just sitting together in silence can remind both of you of the deep bond that defines what it means to be a parent.

What is co-parenting?

Here's the simple truth that I wish someone had shared with me all those years ago:

> Co-parenting is just parenting.

Your role as a parent hasn't changed simply because you're now co-parenting. There will, of course, be changes – perhaps one parent has moved out, your access to your child might not be as frequent and your communication with the other parent may have shifted – but none of this alters the core truth that your role as a parent remains the same.

Your child's expectations of you haven't changed, either. How they look at you, how much they need you and how much they adore you – none of this has changed. Why? Because to your child you are not a co-parent. You are, and always will be, their parent.

Remember during the COVID-19 lockdown, when many of us were asked to work from home? For most of us our bosses still expected us to start at the same time, attend meetings and complete the same tasks. The only thing that changed was the location from which we worked. This, my friend, is co-parenting in a nutshell. The only thing that has changed is the location. Your responsibilities and your child's expectations remain exactly the same.

This love, this bond, does not depend on you and your child's other parent being together, being best friends, or having a perfect relationship. None of that matters when it comes to the relationship between you and your child. Your role is to be there for your child, to lead by example, to love unconditionally and to guide them into adulthood. Everything else is just background noise.

At the end of the day, you are the person they look to for guidance, love and support as they grow. This is the essence of what it means to be a parent and it's the core principle you must remember as you navigate the challenges of raising your child, no matter what the family structure looks like.

Parenting is not dependent on titles like 'co-parent', and your child, depending on their age, probably has no idea what the word means. Many of us don't fully grasp it ourselves – it's something perhaps we only truly come to understand when it's pointed out to us as adults.

REFLECTION: SAME JOB, DIFFERENT SETTING

This exercise will help you appreciate and absorb that, even if your circumstances have changed, your role hasn't.

- Draw two columns on a page. Label one column 'When we were together' and the other 'Now that we're apart'.

- Under each heading, list the responsibilities you had or have as a parent, for example school runs, helping with homework or comforting them when they're upset.
- Then, highlight everything that has stayed the same.

This helps you realise that *co*-parenting doesn't mean less parenting. It's a reminder that the core of your role remains consistent.

#11

Grieving what could have been

For many of you, there was once a picture in your mind of how your family would look.

I had one too.

Mine was probably shaped by my favourite TV shows. A wife, a son and a daughter, a beautiful home with a fridge that had an ice dispenser on the front, and a kitchen big enough for us all to sit down and eat together every night.

That was the dream.

At no point did I imagine being a 40-year-old single man with two sons from two different relationships. But this is my reality.

And here's the truth: dreams and reality don't always meet. And that's okay.

The bigger the dream, the deeper the grief when you realise it won't unfold the way you imagined. There's often a quiet mourning that takes place, not just for the relationship, but for the life you thought you were building.

Sometimes we fight harder to hold on to the dream than we do to accept the reality in front of us.

But separating from the other parent doesn't just end a vision, it creates space for a new one.

The relationship ending doesn't have to mean the end of your happiness.

It doesn't mean the end of you finding your person.

It doesn't mean the end of creating a beautiful family picture.

But it does mean you have to be willing to let go of what was 'supposed to be…' so you can be open to what still can be.

And sometimes, what can be is even greater than what you first imagined.

Part Two

Co-parenting day to day

#12

Navigating the break-up

Redefining your relationship as co-parents rather than former lovers is a critical shift in mindset. It requires understanding that your role now is not to engage in your ex's personal life, but to cooperate in the shared responsibility of parenting.

Here's the truth: you've ended one relationship, but you've begun a new one (*see* 'The co-parenting triangle' on p. 54), a co-parenting partnership that is just as important, if not more so, than your romantic relationship ever was. This new relationship must be grounded in mutual respect and commitment to your child, not control or lingering expectations from your past.

By keeping your focus on the child and maintaining clear, respectful boundaries, you can build a strong co-parenting relationship that serves your child's best interests and allows both parents to thrive in their own personal lives.

When my co-parenting journey began, I struggled with the belief that having a child together gave me the right to information about my co-parent's personal life. I felt I was entitled to know where she was going, who she was speaking to, what her plans were, even on weekends when our child wasn't with her.

This belief was wrong and it led to unnecessary tension. Imagine for a moment that you didn't have a child together. You've broken up with your ex and yet you expect to be kept up to date with their daily activities – where they are going, who they see, what they're doing. Sounds ridiculous, right? Because it is!

In no other type of break-up would this level of involvement be expected or appropriate. Having a child doesn't give you access to the same information or privileges you once had as a romantic partner. The boundaries that exist between ex-partners in a break-up without children should still be respected, even when you're co-parents.

This means you must learn to separate your co-parenting relationship from the intimate relationship you once had. In the intimate phase, you shared emotions, experiences and perhaps every detail of your lives. But once that phase ends and you transition to co-parents, your relationship's core purpose shifts. It's no longer about your emotional needs or desires for connection with each other. It's now solely about raising your child together in a healthy, supportive environment.

What happens in your co-parent's personal life, if it doesn't affect the well-being of your child, is no longer your concern. What you do have a right to know is anything that impacts your child directly. This includes schedules, school events, medical information and other aspects of your child's life that both parents need to be informed about. Clear communication around your shared responsibilities is key, but it must be kept child-focused.

Once I was able to separate the two relationships, my past intimate relationship from my ongoing co-parenting relationship, it made things clearer. It also created space for a healthier, more respectful dynamic between me and my co-parent. We were no longer in conflict over personal matters that didn't involve our child. Instead, we were able to focus on what really mattered – our child's upbringing and well-being.

No negative conversations

Avoid engaging in negative conversations about your previous relationship or your co-parent in general, especially in front of your child. When you dwell on a negative situation, you unintentionally draw more of it into your life. This is why it's crucial to be mindful of the energy and words you put out into the world.

Engaging in conversations about your co-parent or any ex, constantly revisiting the hurt and frustration, will only keep you anchored in discomfort. It prevents healing and creates a barrier between you and the peace you deserve.

Instead, shift your focus to what brings you joy and fulfilment. Redirecting your energy towards growth, gratitude and positivity is the key to moving forward, and breaking free from the emotional weight of the past. This doesn't mean denying your feelings or pretending the hurt never existed; it means choosing not to let it define you.

Rediscovering yourself

It's easy to become so consumed by the role of being a parent that it begins to define you entirely. But being a parent is just one part of who you are, it doesn't erase the person you were before. Yes, you've grown and your responsibilities have changed, but the essence of who you are, your dreams and your individuality are still there, waiting to be embraced.

Ask yourself: in this new chapter of life, who am I? What makes me laugh, what brings me joy and what excites my spirit? Revisit the passions and hobbies you once loved or explore new ones. These aren't luxuries; they are vital to your sense of self. Remember, your identity isn't limited to being a parent, it's enriched by it.

Rediscovering yourself not only brings you fulfilment, but also sets an example for your child that life is about growth, balance and living authentically. Reconnect with your inner self and allow this newfound clarity to guide you into becoming the happiest, most complete version of yourself.

Practise self-love and care

There's a famous quote by Buddha that resonates deeply with me and I felt compelled to include it in this book: 'You yourself, as much as anybody in the entire universe, deserve your love and affection.'

This quote is a powerful reminder that self-love and self-care are necessities.

As a single parent, I understand that every individual's journey is unique. Your support network, challenges and circumstances may look vastly different from someone else's. However, one thing remains universal: the importance of prioritising yourself.

Telling yourself 'I don't have time for me' is a trap that will only keep you confined within a cycle of exhaustion and unhappiness. You cannot pour from an empty cup. Taking time to recharge is not selfish – it's essential for your well-being and your ability to be the best parent you can be.

If possible, carve out moments to step away and recharge. This could mean catching up with friends, taking a quiet walk, reading a book, meditating or indulging in a hobby that brings you joy. Even small, simple acts like eating nourishing meals, staying hydrated and ensuring you get enough sleep can have a profound impact on your mood and energy.

Another helpful approach is to establish a routine that includes time for yourself, even if it's just a few minutes when your child is asleep or otherwise occupied. These moments of solitude can help you reset and feel more balanced, enabling you to tackle parenting challenges with renewed energy and focus.

When you take the time to nurture your own well-being, you're also modelling healthy habits for your child. You're teaching them that self-love and care are integral parts of a fulfilling and balanced life.

Reconnect with friends and community

Spending time with people who uplift and inspire you offers a much-needed escape and serves as a powerful reminder that you are more than just a parent. These moments of connection can reignite your sense of self and provide emotional support during challenging times.

Consider reconnecting with old friends or joining social groups that align with your interests and passions. Building a support network isn't just about companionship – it's about easing the feelings of isolation that can follow a break-up, and surrounding yourself with positivity and encouragement.

During a podcast I recorded with the amazing Jamelia, she shared an invaluable insight: she never had a large village of friends and family around her. But instead of dwelling on what she lacked, she realised she had the power to build that village herself. Her story is a reminder that, while some are fortunate to have a close-knit family who would drop everything at a moment's notice, not everyone is so lucky.

If your family network is limited or non-existent, know that you can create your own 'village' over time. Seek out relationships that are nurturing, genuine and aligned with your values. The bonds you form with others, whether through friendship, community groups or shared experiences, can become just as meaningful and supportive as traditional family ties. Building your village takes effort, but the rewards are immeasurable – a circle of people who lift you up and walk beside you as you navigate life's challenges.

Embrace the future

In this new chapter, you have the power to decide what kind of example you want to set for your child. Rebuilding yourself isn't just for your benefit, it's for theirs too. Your child is learning about relationships by watching you. You're teaching them the importance of self-respect, emotional health and resilience.

Showing them how you rebuild yourself, prioritise self-love and remain focused on the future is an invaluable lesson in resilience. This teaches them that they can navigate hard times and still come out stronger.

Letting go of past hurts isn't about the other parent, it's about your own peace of mind and your child's future. Your ability to move forward, embrace healing and foster a positive co-parenting relationship will shape your child's understanding of love, family and strength.

REFLECTION: REBUILDING WITH INTENTION

This part of your journey isn't only about what's ended, it's about what you choose to build next, for yourself and for your child. Take a quiet moment and consider the following:

▶

- Think about your most recent interactions with your co-parent. Were those conversations truly centred around your child's needs, or did they slip into unresolved feelings or personal frustrations?
- Ask yourself if you're carrying past expectations into your current dynamic. Are you expecting your co-parent to respond as they once did in the relationship, as your intimate partner, instead of who they are now as your co-parent?
- Observe your child. Have you noticed changes in their mood, behaviour or questions since the separation? What might those changes be trying to communicate?
- Consider the week ahead. What's one simple thing you can do to help your child feel more secure, more heard and more loved?

These reflections aren't about blame – they're about building a foundation for growth, understanding and peace. You're not just moving on, you're moving forward.

#13

How children view separation

Separation and co-parenting are global phenomena. Approximately one in four American children live in a single-parent household, according to US Census Bureau data, while in Sweden, shared custody is common, with 35% of children living in dual-residence households after separation. Although the dynamics of separation differ globally, the central challenge remains: ensuring that children are not emotionally scarred by the break-up.

Separation is never easy – not for you and not for your child – and while you adjust to a new chapter, your child is also learning to understand what that shift means for them. Depending on their age and what they've experienced, that understanding will look different.

A child who's never seen their parents together might grow up with different questions. A child who's lived in a two-parent home until age 10 may feel the loss of a familiar rhythm, shared dinners, weekend routines and bedtime hugs from both parents under one roof. These changes can be unsettling and it's okay to acknowledge that.

Children are sensitive to what's happening around them, even when they don't have the language to express it. Your job is not to shield them from the reality of this change, but to help them feel safe during it. This is where your presence, not your perfection, matters most.

When your child sees that, even though things look different, their parents are still showing up with love, consistency and care, it gives them the foundation they need to adjust and thrive. The ending of a relationship doesn't necessarily mean the end of a family – families can look different yet still be deeply loving, secure and connected.

The calm conversations, the open arms, the reassurance that they are still deeply loved are moments that matter more than anything.

Understanding the impact of separation

Separation can leave a deep and lasting mark on children, but its impact varies depending on their age and stage of development. The way children process the breakdown of their parents' relationship is often shaped by their maturity, emotional resilience and understanding of relationships. Let's explore how different age groups experience and respond to the end of their parents' partnership.

Separation before birth

When a couple separates before their child is born, the impact may seem less obvious. However, research suggests that stress during pregnancy can affect the child's development. A November 2023 study from the American Psychological Association highlights that maternal stress is linked to behavioural issues such as anxiety, hyperactivity and conduct disorders in children.

Although the child has not yet formed attachments, they are highly sensitive to the environment into which they are born. Clear communication and a stable co-parenting plan (*see* p. 104) from the start can mitigate future emotional difficulties for both the parents and the child.

The early years

For children under the age of 10, particularly those in the early years (roughly ages two to six), their world is defined by routine and the security provided by their parents. When this familiar structure is disrupted by separation, they may struggle to understand why their world has changed so dramatically.

They can't yet grasp the complexities of adult relationships, but they keenly feel the emotional shifts and changes in their daily lives. Common reactions at this age include increased anxiety, clinginess and a regression to earlier behaviours, such as bed-wetting or tantrums.

Children may even fear that they somehow caused the separation. It's crucial for parents to provide consistent reassurance, explaining the situation in simple, age-appropriate terms and maintaining as much stability as possible in their routines.

Strategies for supporting young Children

Clear communication: Explain the situation in simple terms and be careful not to blame anyone.
Stability in routine: Keep daily activities consistent.
Reassurance: Repeatedly affirm that both parents love the child, even if they are no longer together.

The teenage years

Unlike younger children, teenagers are more likely to understand the reasons behind the separation, yet this understanding doesn't always bring comfort. Instead, it may lead to resentment, loyalty conflicts or even withdrawal from both parents. They might seek independence to cope, pushing boundaries in an attempt to regain control over a life that suddenly feels uncertain.

It's essential for parents to offer teens a safe space to express their feelings without judgement. Open communication is key here, and letting them voice their fears and frustrations can help them process the situation. Involvement in decision-making, such as discussions about custody arrangements, can also give teens a sense of agency, reducing feelings of helplessness. But just as important is maintaining boundaries, ensuring that teenagers understand the separation doesn't give them free rein to act out.

Tips for supporting teenagers

Open dialogue: Create a safe space for them to express their feelings. Avoid making them choose sides.

Involvement in decisions: Including teens in discussions about custody arrangements can help them feel more in control.
Consistent boundaries: Maintain firm and consistent rules in both households.

Adapting to the child in front of you

Every child is unique, and as parents it's essential that we not only recognise that uniqueness, but also adapt our approach to meet each child where they are. There's no one-size-fits-all when it comes to raising a child, just as there isn't in leading a team.

Sir Alex Ferguson, the legendary manager of the English football team Manchester United, was known for his ability to manage different personalities within his squad. He understood that not every player responded well to being shouted at in the dressing room. Some thrived under pressure and direct confrontation – it motivated them – but others would shut down or lose confidence if approached that way. For them, Ferguson knew an arm around the shoulder, a quiet word or a more encouraging tone would bring out their best.

The same applies in parenting. Regardless of how many children you have, the goal is still the same: to raise emotionally secure, resilient and healthy adults. But how you get there will differ from child to child. One may need constant reassurance, while another might value independence. One might learn through conversation, while the other responds better to structure and routine.

Understanding your child's temperament, love language, triggers and motivators allows you to connect more deeply with them, and parent them more effectively. It's not about favouritism or inconsistency, it's about intentionality. When you adjust your parenting to reflect the uniqueness of each child, you're not being soft, you're being strategic. You're creating an environment where they can truly thrive, not just survive.

#14

Why consistency is so important

When two parents make the decision to separate, this new chapter will naturally look and feel different for everyone involved. Yet while the family structure may have shifted, there are still ways to preserve stability for your child without crossing boundaries or giving mixed signals.

That doesn't mean late-night stays at the house or recreating the family dynamic 'for the child's sake'. Unless both parents are genuinely considering a reconciliation, those gestures can blur lines and stir up confusion. Instead, focus on what you can do consistently: school runs, bedtime calls, weekend visits or even just checking in with each other so your child sees that communication and care still exist.

I've already mentioned consistency, but now I want to look at it in more depth, because it is one of the greatest gifts you can offer your child during times of change. It builds trust, creates a sense of safety and helps them feel anchored, even when everything around them feels different.

When plans are regularly cancelled or promises are broken, it doesn't just cause disappointment, it can leave your child feeling confused, questioning their worth and unsure of what to expect. That's why it's so important that both parents, where possible, work to create routines and moments that your child can rely on.

You don't have to be in the same home to be on the same page.

It wasn't the fact that my parents weren't together that impacted me, but the way my dad would drift in and out, never staying long enough for me to trust in his presence. His inconsistency left a deeper scar than I realised. It made me question myself. Was it something I did? Was I not enough to keep him around? I blamed myself for his absence and every time he let me down it felt like a reflection of my own worth.

When a child is left in limbo by one of the people they should be able to rely on the most, it doesn't just create disappointment; it creates doubt – doubt in others, doubt in relationships and, most painfully, doubt in oneself. My dad's inconsistency hurt me, and it shaped the way I viewed my own value, leaving me to carry the burden of wondering why I wasn't important enough to stay for.

That's why what matters most is that your child feels seen, valued and secure – not because things have stayed the same at home, but because love, reliability and care from both their parents remains constant, no matter the circumstances.

Maintaining and creating routines

Think about the activities and routines you shared with your child before the separation. Did you have regular outings like taking them to football practice, going for walks or doing special activities together? It's important to continue these activities as much as possible, despite the separation.

Familiar routines provide a sense of stability and security, which is especially important for children during times of upheaval. By maintaining these routines you reinforce the message that the separation is not their fault and that your love for them is unwavering. Routine is a comforting reminder that their relationship with you remains constant.

In addition to preserving old routines, you can use this time to create new ones that further strengthen your bond. For instance, if you haven't done this before, consider introducing a monthly 'special meal' where you and your child go out to eat together or make something special at home.

Depending on their age, this can be an opportunity not only to have fun, but also to create a safe space for open, personal conversations. During these meals, share what you're feeling or experiencing (in an age-appropriate way) and encourage your child to do the same. Let them know that it's okay to talk about their emotions and that you are always there to listen without judgement.

By maintaining old routines and creating new ones you help your child feel secure and supported, minimising their fears of abandonment or blame. You also create regular opportunities for connection, reinforcing your relationship during this challenging time.

#15

The power of reassurance

Seeking reassurance in any relationship is normal. In fact, our need for it becomes even louder during moments of doubt or instability. Think about the times you've had tension with a partner or close friend:

- An argument that left you unsure where you stood
- A rocky patch that made you question their commitment
- A moment of disrespect that changed how safe you felt
- Or an even deeper wound, like betrayal.

Now think about how your mind works during those moments, sending you negative thoughts and doubts:

- What does this mean for us?
- Are we going to be okay?
- Is this the beginning of the end?

These moments of uncertainty can leave you feeling anxious and extremely unsettled. You begin to reflect on recent interactions, reread messages you sent to see if you were at fault, overthink their silence. These behaviours can build and build – and that's as adults with life experience, developed brains and better emotional understanding.

Now imagine being a child trying to process these same feelings during their moments of uncertainty, such as:

- **Parents splitting up:** One home becomes two, and suddenly their whole world is being reorganised.
- **A parent disappearing or being inconsistent:** One week they show up with hugs and promises; the next week they're nowhere to be found.
- **Plans and routines changing at the last minute:** Bags are packed, excitement is building, but then they're told, 'It's not happening today.'
- **A new partner appearing:** A stranger is suddenly sharing their space, their parent's attention, and their world.

For a child, these moments shake the foundation of their security. So if we as adults need reassurance after conflict, uncertainty or emotional shock, imagine just how much more a child needs.

Reassurance in any relationship can take different forms, depending on the needs of the individual. Some of us require verbal reassurance, such as 'I love you' or 'I'm always here for you' and 'Nothing has changed between us.' These words can mean so much to those who need it.

For others, verbal reassurance may not do much at all and it's physical reassurance that is required, such as hugging and showing up in person. Being present provides that extra layer of comfort for your child, but without reassurance in any relationship it's difficult to know where someone stands.

As co-parents, reassurance must become one of our greatest tools and responsibilities, because no matter how resilient children are, they're still just that – children. They internalise change. They question silence. And they often blame themselves for things that are completely out of their control.

I remember vividly when Tyler's mum got married. He must've only been around five years old when he shared a dream with me that left a lasting impression. He said in the dream he was at his mum's wedding, but then someone told him he was never going to see me again. He woke up upset, confused and unsettled. At just five years old, his little heart and mind were already trying to make sense of big, adult shifts.

The fact that he felt safe enough to share that dream with me was, in itself, a beautiful moment and a reminder that even young children carry deep thoughts and emotional burdens, and they look to us, not for all the answers, but for safety.

In that moment I knew my role wasn't to analyse or dismiss, it was simply to reassure. I told him that his mum getting married was a beautiful thing. That now he had an even bigger family, filled with more people who loved him and wanted to see him thrive. But above all, I made sure he understood this: 'No matter what happens, I will always be here. You can see me whenever you want. All you have to do is ask.'

In that one conversation, I was able to do two incredibly important things:

1. Normalise and celebrate the changes happening in his world.
2. Reaffirm my role in his life as something unchangeable and unshakable.

Depending on when your separation or break-up happened, your child may have unanswered questions or unresolved emotions. They may look at other families and wonder why theirs doesn't look the same. They may see both parents show up at a friend's school play, but only one of you at theirs. They may notice the absence of your voice on certain mornings or the quiet at the dinner table.

These moments, if left unchecked, don't just hurt, they shape. Without reassurance, children can develop silent insecurities:

- Does my dad not love me any more?
- Am I not important enough for both my parents to be around?
- What did I do wrong?

And the longer those doubts live in the dark, the deeper they root. That's why reassurance isn't just about saying 'I love you' or 'I'll always be here.' It's about:

- Showing up consistently, even in small ways
- Answering hard questions with honesty wrapped in empathy
- Naming the emotions they may be too afraid to express themselves.

It's about anchoring your child when everything else around them is shifting and out of their control.

Questions to ask yourself as a co-parent

- Have I reassured my child lately about my presence in their life? Or am I assuming they 'just know'?
- When big life changes happen, like remarriage, moving house, new siblings, do I take time to check in with my child emotionally or just inform them of the facts?
- What unspoken fears might my child be carrying about our family dynamic?
- Do I make space for them to express emotions without fear of being shut down, dismissed or guilt-tripped?
- Am I showing up for them in a way that feels consistent, not just convenient?

Reassurance is not a one-time thing. It's a practice.

> It's the quiet nod you give them across the room.
>
> It's the phone call you always answer.
>
> It's the promise you make and keep.

In a world where families can take many shapes, your presence, backed by words and actions of love, is the constant they will carry with them for life.

#16

Is your child torn?

Imagine you have two friends who are no longer speaking to each other. Where there was once joy and laughter, only tension and negativity remain. You feel great affection for both, but you don't know what to say to them or how to be with them. You worry about being disloyal, and hearing them criticise each other only makes things worse, so perhaps you distance yourself from them both to avoid having to choose sides.

Now, imagine how a child feels during their parents' separation. They have the same overwhelming emotions, but at a much younger age and with less understanding of why everything has changed. They feel torn between the two people they love most and this is happening inside their own home, where they normally feel safe and secure.

It's crucial to understand that children must be shielded from the emotional fallout of separation. They are not equipped to handle adult conflicts and involving them in your hurt, anger or frustration only burdens them with emotions they aren't ready to process. When parents allow their pain to overshadow the needs of their child, it creates confusion and insecurity. This is why it's important for both parents to remain focused on the well-being of the child.

By placing your personal feelings aside and prioritising your child's emotional stability you can help them cope more effectively. It's about ensuring that, despite the breakdown of the relationship, the child still feels loved and supported by both parents. Maintaining clear boundaries between personal issues and your role as a parent creates a space where the child can continue to grow and thrive.

Research shows that children who experience cooperative co-parenting have better emotional outcomes. With the right support, children can emerge from separation emotionally resilient and capable of forming healthy relationships. This support comes in the form of clear communication, emotional stability and a continued relationship with both parents.

Ensuring children know they are loved unconditionally and that the separation was not their fault can significantly lessen the emotional toll. As a co-parent, it's essential to focus on what remains constant: your role as a parent and the unconditional love you provide.

Ideal homes

Children can often feel the weight of the environment they step into. If one home always has the essentials and the other feels unprepared, the child may notice this long before the parents do. They may not say anything, but inside they begin to associate one home with comfort, organisation and safety, and the other with uncertainty or lack.

That imbalance can quietly shape how secure they feel in each space. This is why it's important for both homes to have the basics. Now I didn't say luxuries. We are simply talking about essentials here:

- Pyjamas
- Underwear
- Toothbrush
- Spare clothes
- Basic medicines
- Food they like

These are the everyday things a child shouldn't have to worry about needing. When they aren't available, the child can feel put in a very difficult position, where they are the one who must remember, pack and carry everything between homes.

Imagine your child being ill and coming to stay with you, but you don't have the basics to comfort them – no blanket, no spare pyjamas, no Calpol, not even their favourite nourishing food. In that moment, it's not the illness that creates the insecurity, it's the feeling that you weren't prepared for them.

It is not the responsibility of one parent to provide all the essentials for both homes. As adults, it's our role to ensure that when our child walks through the door they don't have to wonder whether their needs will be met. Having the essentials in both homes doesn't mean they need to be equipped identically. It simply means your child can relax, settle and be a child.

It means they aren't silently comparing the two homes and feeling guilty, anxious or unsettled when one lacks the basics the other has. When both parents commit to this as a minimum, the child moves between homes without fear of 'going without'. They experience consistency, stability and care, not the feeling of being stuck in the middle of who did or didn't provide what.

Who is it for?

I've seen many parents clash over items not being sent back, items not being allowed to travel between homes and even items mysteriously going 'missing'. But when you look closely, these situations often reveal something deeper: the item was more about the adult than it was about the child.

We buy something for our child, yet we decide where they can take it, when they can wear it and which home it 'belongs' to. Now, I'm not suggesting that TVs, PlayStations or big-ticket items need to travel from house to house. That's unrealistic. But if you're a parent who buys your child an expensive pair of trainers and they only get to wear them once, because you want to be seen as the parent with the 'nice things' at your house, then let's be honest, that item was never about the child. It was about you.

My mindset is simple. If I've bought something for my child, I want them to get the most wear, joy and comfort out of it, wherever they are. A child shouldn't have to think twice before picking up their favourite T-shirt, teddy or shoes because one parent might have an issue with it travelling.

But I also want to acknowledge something important. There are parents out there who will be spiteful regardless. They won't return items that have been sent. They may force you to repeatedly replace things while refusing to contribute financially. Some will expect their monthly contribution, if they even pay that, to stretch far beyond what it realistically covers.

In situations like this, boundaries become necessary. You cannot be blamed for refusing to send items you simply cannot afford to keep rebuying. Protecting your financial stability and avoiding repeated loss is not the same as using items to punish the other parent. It is a practical response to someone else's behaviour, but you need to know the difference. Are you holding back items out of spite or out of genuine necessity because the other parent refuses to act in good faith? When the item truly is for the child, their needs, comfort and happiness come first, not our pride, frustration or need to compete with the other parent, and when boundaries are truly needed, they are about protection, not punishment.

REFLECTION: AM I PUTTING MY CHILD IN THE MIDDLE?

Take a few minutes to answer these questions honestly. Reflect on your behaviours and how they impact your child.

Messages and conflicts

- Do you expect your child to carry messages between homes?
- Do you involve them in conflicts that are between adults?
- How does this make your child feel and what could you do differently to protect them from adult issues?

Items and comfort

- Have you ever restricted a comfort item, clothing or toy to your home out of pride, control or competition?
- Are your boundaries about necessity and fairness or about ego or spite?
- How can you ensure your child has what they need in both homes without placing them in the middle?

▶

Intentions behind purchases

- When you buy something for your child, what is the intention behind it?
- Is it genuinely for their comfort, joy or growth?
- How can you shift your mindset so that your purchases serve your child's needs first, not your pride?

If you notice areas where your child's needs could be prioritised more, write down one small adjustment you could make. For example:

- Allow a comfort item to travel freely between homes.
- Communicate directly with the other parent instead of relying on your child.
- Adjust your purchasing or sharing habits so your child benefits most.

Reflecting on small changes like these can lift a huge weight from your child's shoulders and create a healthier, more stable environment across both homes.

#17

Establishing boundaries

Boundaries are often the one thing many co-parents struggle to put in place, especially in the early stages of separation. This isn't because people don't care. More often it's because they're navigating unfamiliar territory, caught between grief, guilt, fear of conflict or a deep desire to 'keep the peace' for the sake of the child. But here's the truth: real peace can't exist without boundaries. So, before we go any further, let's start by defining what a boundary really is, without the emotional weight or assumptions.

A boundary is a limit or guideline that protects your emotional, mental and sometimes physical well-being. It's how we teach others how to treat us and how we honour ourselves. Take a moment and sit with that. Does it feel selfish? Harsh? Unfair? Many people associate boundaries with rejection or control, but in reality boundaries are a form of love. They protect the space where healthy relationships can grow, especially after the emotional landscape of a break-up.

To better understand this, think about the boundaries we all accept without question in everyday life:

- A 20mph speed limit near a school is there to protect lives, especially those of children crossing the road.
- Age restrictions on alcohol and smoking exist to safeguard young people until they're ready to make informed adult decisions.

We rarely see these boundaries as 'unfair'; we see them as necessary. They're not about control – they're about care. So why should emotional boundaries be any different?

Boundaries within relationships

Boundaries in co-parenting might look different from traffic laws or age limits, but their purpose is the same: to create safety, respect and clarity. Setting boundaries doesn't mean you're shutting the other parent out; it means you're defining what's needed for you both to show up in the healthiest way possible for your child. Boundaries say:

- This is how I can engage without burning out.
- This is what helps me stay focused on our child, rather than our past.

In friendships, a boundary might look like setting limits on how much time you spend with a particular friend in order to maintain your own mental health. I'm sure I am not the only one who has had to pull back from certain friends at times, because of the impact it was having on my own mental well-being. In a business environment, it could mean establishing work hours and refusing to answer emails after those hours, to protect your work-life balance. And, of course, in co-parenting, boundaries ensure that communication and interactions remain respectful and focused on the well-being of the child.

The misconception is that boundaries are harsh or selfish, but they are healthy and necessary for every type of relationship. They prevent resentment, build respect and create clear expectations about how you wish to be treated. When people respect your boundaries, it's a sign that they respect you. Boundaries aren't just about controlling others, they're about protecting yourself and building healthier, more sustainable relationships.

Contemplating boundary-setting

You may be reading this thinking that you and your co-parent don't need boundaries. Maybe you're going on family holidays, having late-night discussions or even have an open-door policy at each other's homes. This might be working for now, but one thing I often ask people to consider is this: if your co-parenting relationship would have to change if one of you started dating someone new, then your co-parenting relationship probably needs boundaries now.

It's not about spite – it's about protecting your peace and preventing future tension. By setting boundaries early, you create a healthier, more stable dynamic for both co-parents and the child involved. In my many conversations with my followers, my therapist and through reflecting on my own journey, I've learned a few key things that I want to share with you.

If you've been debating whether to set a boundary, chances are you should have already set one. That constant back-and-forth we experience in our minds is a sign that we're not happy. We might feel uncomfortable, yet we worry about how the other person will feel and how it may impact the child, rather than ensuring we are safe, comfortable and at ease. Remember, if you're feeling uncomfortable, stressed or low, your child will likely pick up on this energy, even if you think you're hiding it well.

Sometimes, we tolerate things we know aren't right for us because we don't want to make waves. We avoid taking action for fear of making the wrong move, and the result is we end up stuck. Think of quicksand: the longer you remain in it, the harder it becomes to pull yourself out.

Boundaries don't stop you being a good parent

In the early years of co-parenting, my child's mum and I argued regularly, and a lot of it was due to my desire for control. I wanted the same access and involvement I had when we were together, but the reality of co-parenting felt very different. Each month, I had to pay the amount the Child Maintenance Service told me to pay, which added to the sense that I had little say in how things were being handled. On top of that, I felt like my time with my child was dictated by someone else. It felt like everything was out of my hands and I struggled with that. But here's the thing: it wasn't a game where someone had the upper hand, it was real life.

Co-parenting isn't about 'winning', it's about working together for the sake of your child. That's something I had to come to terms with, and I know many of you might be feeling the same frustration right now.

In those early days, I didn't have a clear example of what co-parenting looked like. I hadn't even seen two parents raise a child together, let alone co-parent effectively. So, like many of you might be doing, I was figuring it out as I went, making a lot of mistakes along the way.

At one point, my child's mother stopped answering my calls. I immediately assumed she was doing it to be difficult or to spite me. I pointed the finger at her, not stopping to think about her reasons. What I didn't realise was that she wasn't avoiding me out of malice, she was protecting her peace. Our constant arguing was mentally exhausting for her and stepping back was her way of preserving her emotional well-being.

Another boundary she put in place was asking me to pick up our child from his grandma's house, so we wouldn't have to meet face-to-face and risk unnecessary conflict. Did I agree with the boundary? No. Did I like it? Definitely not. But did I respect it? Yes. And here's the thing:

- Did this boundary stop me from seeing my child? **No.**
- Did it hurt my relationship with my child? **Not at all.**
- Did it help keep the peace and make things easier for my child's mum? **Absolutely.**

This is something I want you to reflect on. If you're feeling frustrated by boundaries being put in place, ask yourself: are they really stopping me from being a good parent?

I've heard from many of you who say, 'But my child's other parent wouldn't agree to this.' And here's my thought: if a boundary like this, designed to minimise conflict, would cause someone to stop seeing their child or constantly cancel plans, I'd argue that person wasn't very committed to seeing their child in the first place.

Regardless of the boundaries placed on me, whether I thought they were fair or not, I remained consistent with my child. None of these boundaries stopped me from being a present parent. They weren't there to keep me away or to spite me; they were there to protect our peace and, ultimately, that helped us create a healthier environment for our child.

Proactive versus reactive

One of the common mistakes we make in co-parenting is setting boundaries only after things have already gone wrong. These are what I call reactive boundaries. For example, you and your co-parent might frequently argue over the phone, so you decide to communicate only through text to avoid conflict. While this boundary can help, it was only set in response to something negative happening.

But what if this boundary had been in place from the start? It might have prevented the arguments altogether. This is the power of proactive boundaries, because they set clear expectations before issues arise, and protect both parents and, ultimately, the child.

Now reactive boundaries can still be useful, but what if we focus on setting proactive boundaries instead? For example, at the beginning of your co-parenting journey, you might consider setting a boundary where communication is limited to discussions about the child and only takes place during agreed-upon hours between, say, 8 a.m. and 7 p.m.

While it may feel uncomfortable at first, as you may worry how the other parent might perceive you, over time this boundary can significantly contribute to a more peaceful environment. This approach keeps communication child-focused and ensures that both parents are mentally prepared for discussions, helping to avoid emotional overflow that can happen during unplanned or late-night conversations. It also respects each parent's time and personal space.

Now, this type of boundary may not be necessary for everyone. In some co-parenting relationships, communication is naturally respectful and strict guidelines aren't required. However, in situations where there's lingering emotional tension, or one parent feels overwhelmed, boundaries like this can be invaluable. Sometimes, after a break-up, we remain too familiar with our co-parent. Depending on when and how the relationship ended, one or both of you may still need time to heal.

When you're co-parenting, you don't have the luxury of moving on without contact, because you have a child together. But one of you may be more impacted by the break-up than the other. Perhaps one parent desires to get back together while the other is ready to move on. In these cases, maintaining regular, emotionally neutral communication can be difficult.

Proactive boundaries allow both parents to create a better environment for everyone concerned. These boundaries help both of you exist more peacefully, individually and as a family unit, as you move forward. By setting boundaries early, you give yourselves the space to heal and adjust to the new dynamic, making your co-parenting partnership more effective and less emotionally charged.

If someone reacts negatively to your boundary and shows a lack of respect, it's a clear sign that the boundary was necessary. People who love, respect and care for you will also respect your boundaries. Remember, a boundary is not meant to spite anyone, but to protect you. If you set it with that mindset, trust in your decision and know that you're doing the right thing.

Boundaries are not temporary

When things start improving after a boundary has been put in place, it's easy to think, 'Great, everything's fine now. Maybe I can loosen up.' This is a mistake that many people make: thinking that because things are going smoothly they no longer need the boundary. But that's a sign that your boundaries are working, so why would you remove them?

Think of it like placing a fence around your garden to stop dogs from ruining your flowers. After a few months, your flowers are thriving and you might think, 'It's been a while since a dog has trampled my flowers, so maybe I don't need this fence any more.' But that would be a mistake, wouldn't it?

The only reason your flowers have been safe is because the fence is there. If you take it down, the very problems you were trying to avoid could start happening all over again. Boundaries function in the same way. They're not a temporary fix; they are a long-term strategy to keep your life and your relationships healthy and balanced. The moment you start loosening or removing them because things are 'going well', you risk falling back into old patterns that made the boundary necessary in the first place.

This doesn't mean that boundaries are rigid or can never change. As situations evolve, it's natural to reassess and tweak them to suit new circumstances. But the idea that you should remove them altogether just because things have improved is like removing the fence around your garden because it's been successful. Things are going well because the boundary is there.

Boundaries don't have to be announced

As I mentioned earlier, when my son was young, after his mother and I separated, I found myself constantly calling her. I wanted to know what she was doing, where she was going and who she was with. Often, I would use our son as an excuse to reach out, asking questions under the guise of concern for his well-being.

I would even call when I had him – not because it was necessary, but because I wanted to keep tabs on her. Looking back, I can see that what I was really doing was trying to control a situation that was no longer mine to control.

As time went on, she stopped answering my calls. Instead, she only responded to text messages related to our son. There was no formal conversation, no warning where she explained that she was setting a boundary.

At first, her lack of response drove me mad. In my mind I was justified to call. It could have been an emergency. Why wasn't she answering? It took me a while to connect the dots, but eventually I realised that I was wasting my energy. Every ignored call left me more frustrated, but the frustration wasn't her doing, it was mine.

Looking back at those messages I cringe, because I can see I was essentially arguing with myself – message after message from me, with no response from her.

It's important to understand that boundaries don't need to be communicated or justified, they simply need to be upheld. My son's mother never told me she was setting boundaries and she didn't have to. By consistently refusing to engage with anything that wasn't about our son, she showed me where her line was. And, over time, I came to respect it.

As childish as it seems now, I know many of you reading this have either done the same or had it done to you. My hope in being vulnerable and sharing this is that it resonates with you and encourages a change in how you approach your relationships. Boundaries are not about control; they're about protecting your peace and focusing on what truly matters. What I learned through this experience was that my priority should have always been our son.

- Was I still able to see him? **Yes.**
- Was he healthy and happy? **Yes.**

That's what mattered. If his mother had engaged with me every time I pushed, I might have never come to that realisation. Sometimes, silence forces us to reflect on our own behaviour. A man's role as a father should never be dependent on how much access he has to the mother. Once I accepted that, I was able to focus on being a better father and co-parent.

Setting your boundaries

I can't tell you exactly which boundaries to implement, but here are some key areas to focus on:

Keep personal lives separate and stay child-focused
To foster a healthy co-parenting relationship, the expectations and informality of your former intimate relationship can no longer exist. Instead, focus on working together respectfully for the child.

Your ex doesn't need to know every detail of your life and vice versa
It's important to establish boundaries that limit discussions to your child. Stick to the essentials and avoid delving into each other's personal lives.

Avoid discussing relationship matters – focus solely on your child
Conversations should be about the well-being and needs of your child. Rehashing relationship issues will only complicate things.

Create a consistent routine for your child
Having a set schedule allows everyone, especially the child, to feel more secure. It also reduces the need for constant back-and-forth discussions about arrangements.

Prioritise one-on-one time with your child, not time as a family
Your child needs to adjust to the new dynamic. Continuing to spend time as a 'family' can confuse them and make it harder for both parents to move on.

Once these boundaries are set, they will become a natural part of your co-parenting relationship. It may take time to adjust, but consistency is key. If you're not firm with these boundaries, you risk slipping back into old habits from your previous intimate relationship.

This is where confusion arises, particularly for the child. However, children are resilient. They will adapt to the new dynamic as long as both parents remain respectful and consistent. Remember, your child loves both their parents and wants them to be actively involved in their lives.

Setting healthy co-parenting boundaries can significantly impact how you show up for your child and help them thrive in a two-home environment.

Your rights in setting boundaries

- You have the right to say no without feeling guilty.
- You have the right to be treated with respect.
- You have the right to make your needs as important as the needs of others.
- You have the right not to meet other people's expectations.

Honouring these rights will help you find peace and comfort as you move forward.

REFLECTION: WHERE WOULD BOUNDARIES BE BENEFICIAL?

After reading this chapter, take some uninterrupted time to reflect on your current co-parenting situation.

- Ask yourself: where in my co-parenting relationship do I feel tension, discomfort or emotional exhaustion?
  Write down one or two specific moments or recurring situations that come to mind.
- Then, for each, ask yourself: what boundary could I put in place to protect my peace and support a healthier environment for my child.'
  I don't want you to think about how the other person might respond. Instead focus on what you need to feel respected, safe and stable.
  Remember, not every boundary needs to be announced to the world. Some are simply about how you choose to respond, what you give your energy to or what you no longer opt to engage with.
- After you've identified these boundaries, consider whether any of them do need to be communicated and, if so, how you can do so clearly and calmly to create clarity, mutual respect and a more stable environment for everyone involved.

#18

Co-parenting with intentionality

Even parents who are in a relationship or married aren't always aligned on what they want for their child, so it's no surprise that parents who are no longer together and are co-parenting can often find themselves at odds, too. For example:

- One parent might dream of their child becoming a footballer, while the other envisions them pursuing law.
- One might feel strongly that the child shouldn't date until they are 18, while the other takes a more relaxed approach.
- One might follow a vegan diet and want the child to do the same, while the other has been eating meat all their life and sees nothing wrong with this.

These differences in opinion are normal. You're two different people with different upbringings, values and perspectives. But despite the differences in how you believe your child should get there, your goal is the same: raising a healthy, secure and well-rounded adult.

Why goals matter

It isn't about saying yes to avoid tantrums or making sure they never feel disappointment. It's about having a clear target. Imagine a basketball team running up and down the court with no hoops. How exhausted would they get? How pointless would the game feel?

More importantly, how would you ever measure their success? This is parenting without a goal.

Acknowledging that your goal is to raise a healthy adult gives you confidence in the choices you make today. It allows you to say no with certainty, knowing that short-term discomfort is sometimes necessary for long-term growth. It helps you recognise harmful patterns and break cycles that could negatively shape your child's future.

In almost every other area of life we set intentions and create goals, because we understand that direction gives us purpose and purpose shapes our decisions. Think about it. If someone wants to become an electrician, once they've identified that goal, they pursue the relevant training, complete the required hours, and make sure their time and energy are spent in alignment with that path. It wouldn't make sense for them to suddenly enrol on an accounting course, because it doesn't serve the goal they've set.

Or take someone whose goal is to improve their health and fitness. They know it requires a level of discipline. They become mindful of their food choices, cut back on alcohol and commit to regular exercise. Every action becomes intentional, because it's tied to a larger purpose. When we set goals as parents, we begin to ask better questions:

- Does this choice support the kind of child I want to raise?
- Does this routine support their development?
- Does this discipline style align with the future I want for my child?

Co-parenting, however, often requires even more intentionality, because you're not under the same roof. You don't have the luxury of daily conversations, quick check-ins or being able to make decisions together in the moment. That's why the foundations that guide how you both show up as parents need to be strong, especially when emotions run high or circumstances change.

They become what they see

Once you've set your parenting goals, you need to make every action intentional, too, because children are not passive observers; they are constantly learning from the environment around them. Your child is building their understanding of love, safety and self-worth based on what they witness day after day. And, while no parent is perfect, it's worth asking yourself what your child might be learning from you.

The energy in the home, the way conflicts are handled, how love is shown (or withheld), and even the silence between arguments all leave lasting impressions. Our actions and behaviours are shaping our child as a future adult, so these are some of the things that should be avoided:

- **Inconsistency:** A child who never knows what to expect (emotionally or physically) may grow into an adult who struggles with attachment. They might crave security, but push people away out of fear of abandonment.
- **Constant arguments:** A child raised in a home full of conflict may end up in unhealthy relationships, believing that love and chaos go hand in hand. They may repeat the patterns they saw, normalising dysfunction.
- **Using them as a messenger:** A child caught in the middle of adult issues may grow into an adult who struggles with boundaries. They may feel responsible for other people's emotions, leading to people-pleasing or unhealthy relationships.
- **Emotional neglect:** A child who isn't allowed to express their emotions may become an adult who suppresses their feelings, struggles with self-worth or avoids intimacy.
- **Lack of accountability:** If a child never sees an apology or accountability from a parent, they may grow into an adult who either struggles to own their mistakes or accepts mistreatment, because they were never taught what a healthy apology looks like.

You are helping to shape a future adult every single day, whether you realise it or not, so instead of focusing on battling your co-parent, or trying to outdo them by winning your child over with temporary happiness, ask yourself: what am I teaching them about love, trust and stability? What patterns am I passing down? Because the true measure of your success as a parent (not co-parent) won't be how happy they were as a child, it will be how healthy they are as an adult.

Looking back on your own childhood, would you say your parents did a good job in raising you? Whatever your answer, take a moment to think about why. If your answer is yes, what made the difference? Was it because you had fun as a child, were spoiled with gifts, taken on amazing getaways, or covered with love and protection? Or was it because you felt safe, heard and emotionally supported?

If your answer is no, was it because you lacked those things? Or is it because, as an adult, you now recognise the traumas you carry? Memories that still affect you today based on what you witnessed as a child? Did the arguments, instability or emotional neglect shape the way you view relationships, trust or your own self-worth?

The reason I ask this is to highlight an important truth: as parents, not just co-parents, our goal should always be to raise a healthy adult, not just a happy child; a person who can move through life without being burdened by unresolved childhood trauma; a person who is emotionally secure, self-sufficient and not held back by wounds they didn't ask for. This has nothing to do with how many parents are in the household. It has everything to do with what is being witnessed under that roof.

REFLECTION: EMBODYING YOUR INTENTION

Now the following may be a short question, but the response requires some depth, so take some time to sit with it and answer it honestly.

- Ask yourself: what kind of adult do I want my child to become? Write a short paragraph or even a few bullet points describing the qualities, values and emotional strengths you hope they will carry into adulthood. For example, you might want them to be confident, empathetic, resilient, emotionally secure, kind, independent and so on.
- Once you've defined those qualities, ask yourself: am I currently modelling these qualities in the way I parent? For example:
  * If you want your child to be emotionally secure, are you emotionally available and consistent with your love and support?

▶

  * If you want them to handle conflict well, do they see you resolving disagreements calmly, especially with your co-parent?
- Don't judge yourself. If you realise you're not modelling some of the values you hope to instil, take a moment to celebrate that awareness. That realisation is powerful. It's not a failure; it's an opportunity for growth. The goal isn't perfection. It's intention.
- From here, choose one small way you can better reflect one of those values in the coming week. Write it down and commit to trying it.

#19

With due respect

For some of you, having respect for your co-parent may feel like an impossible ask. Especially if their behaviour has been toxic, inconsistent or downright hurtful. But hear me out: this isn't about excusing the past, it's about leading with intention, protecting your peace and being there for your child in a way that breaks cycles, not repeats them.

Some of us show up to work every day, facing bosses or colleagues we don't particularly like. We might be spoken to with a tone we don't appreciate, handed tasks that feel unfair or placed in uncomfortable situations, yet we still manage to maintain professionalism and respect. Why? Because we understand what's at stake. We know that if we respond recklessly, we could lose our job, our income, our security. That awareness keeps us in check.

Now ask yourself this: if I can extend that level of self-control and maturity in a work environment for the sake of a paycheck, why can't I do the same with my co-parent for the sake of our child? You're not risking a job, you're risking your child's emotional well-being, sense of safety and relationship with both parents. That should be an even greater incentive to lead with respect, even when it's not easy.

Respectful co-parenting isn't just about avoiding conflict. It's about creating a stable, nurturing environment for your child to thrive. When respect is prioritised:

- Your child benefits from a harmonious co-parenting dynamic, reducing their stress and uncertainty.
- You provide a model for handling relationships with dignity and cooperation.
- Both parents can focus on the shared goal of raising a happy, well-adjusted child.

Having respect doesn't mean you have to be best friends with your co-parent. It doesn't even mean you have to like them. What it does mean is treating them with the basic courtesy you'd expect in return.

Even when they're behaving in ways you deem disrespectful, it's important not to stoop to their level or fight fire with fire. Your child is always watching and absorbing how you interact with their other parent. These interactions set the tone for how they will approach relationships in the future. Do you want your child to grow up thinking disrespect and conflict are normal in relationships? Or would you rather they learn the value of empathy, communication and cooperation?

Ask yourself: what does stooping to my co-parent's level really achieve? Yes, it might feel good in the moment, but if your goal is to raise a happy, healthy child, then showing respect or at least modelling it yourself becomes one of the most impactful lessons you can teach your child.

It needs to be mutual

Running the @Raisingboys2Men platform means I interact with countless co-parents every day, hearing their stories and witnessing the challenges they face. Many of these interactions highlight situations where respect is completely absent. People often share their frustrations through comments or direct messages, sometimes publicly, filled with anger about their co-parent's behaviour.

But here's the thing: the language they use to describe the other parent often reveals just as much about the dynamics of the relationship as the actions they're describing. When I see harsh or even foul language being used, it becomes clear that respect isn't just missing from one side, it's likely a mutual issue.

You can often get a sense of who might be contributing to the problem simply by paying attention to how each parent speaks about the other. Respect doesn't excuse bad behaviour, but it does set a tone. When it's absent, it can create a cycle of blame and hostility that ultimately harms the child caught in the middle.

In situations like these, the child often suffers the most. They struggle with anxiety, insecurity, and divided loyalties, unsure how to process the tension between their parents. It's heartbreaking and it's avoidable.

Respect is a cornerstone of any healthy relationship and it's no different in co-parenting. This isn't just about avoiding conflict, it's about creating a positive example for your child. When a child see their parents treating each other with respect, even in difficult circumstances, they learn how to handle disagreements, communicate effectively and collaborate with others.

Mutual respect also has practical benefits. It makes the logistics of co-parenting smoother, leading to better communication, more effective problem-solving and a more harmonious environment for everyone involved. Even small gestures, like being punctual, polite or communicating well in advance if you need to change an arrangement, can make a significant difference.

Respect isn't always easy, especially when emotions are running high or past hurts linger, but it's a choice. It's a commitment to prioritising your child's well-being over temporary feelings of anger or resentment. And in making that choice you're not just respecting the other parent, you're respecting your child and the future you want for them.

Let's explore some thought-provoking ways to evaluate and deepen respect in your co-parenting relationship by asking yourself the following questions:

How honest are your conversations? When communicating with your co-parent, are you sharing essential information about your child's well-being with clarity and openness? Are you listening to their concerns, especially when they relate to your child?

Do you honour their time? Being punctual for pick-ups and drop-offs isn't just courteous, it demonstrates that you value your child's routine and respect their need for consistency.

What tone are you setting for your child? Do your words about your co-parent build your child's sense of security, or could they create confusion or distress? Remember, your child absorbs the dynamics between you and their other parent.

Are you modelling healthy relationships? The way you interact with your co-parent teaches your child valuable lessons about respect, conflict resolution and collaboration. Are your current interactions and behaviours providing a positive example?

Is your child protected from adult issues? Are you shielding your child from unnecessary exposure to disagreements, negative comments or stressful situations? Protecting their emotional environment is a profound act of respect.

Are you supporting your child's relationship with their other parent? Do your actions encourage a strong, loving bond between your child and your co-parent, even when it's difficult? Your child's connection to both parents is vital to their sense of self and security.

Are your actions truly as respectful as they could be? What's one small change you can make today to better align with your shared goal of raising a thriving child? Taking a clear-sighted look at your behaviour in the past can be a good way of thinking about how you might improve it in the future, which is what this exercise helps you do.

REFLECTION: THE (UNSENT) ACCOUNTABILITY LETTER

The aim of this exercise is to help you practise emotional honesty without the pressure of a real-time confrontation. By writing a letter you're creating a safe space to reflect on your own actions without fear, defensiveness or judgement.

- Write a letter to your co-parent acknowledging your role in a past argument or disrespectful exchange.
- You don't have to send this, but working it through in writing can shift how you hold yourself going forward.
- Take ownership of your actions and behaviour, but don't justify; just reflect.
- End the letter with one change you are committed to making.

I understand that it takes a lot to be the bigger person, especially when the other parent is being disrespectful or difficult. However, your child is worth those moments of swallowed pride and personal growth. This exercise helps you develop that growth even further by encouraging you to revisit a past conflict or disrespectful exchange with your co-parent not just from your perspective, but through the eyes of your child. This isn't about blame. It's about becoming the kind of parent who owns their actions, learns from them and leads by example.

REFLECTION: THE PLAYBACK TEST

- Think of a time when communication between you and your co-parent became disrespectful, through text, in person or over the phone.
- Now imagine your child at age 16 being shown a recording of your actions or messages in that moment.
- Write down what you think they'd feel. Would they be proud, disappointed, confused? What message would your behaviour have taught them about relationships?

#20

Parenting plans

A parenting plan is a voluntary, written agreement between co-parents that outlines how they will raise their child together, even while living apart. This approach is not about controlling the other parent, but creating a roadmap for the child's well-being.

Depending on how the relationship ended and the attitudes of both parents, co-parenting after separation can be challenging, with emotions often running high, but a well-thought-out parenting plan can help bring clarity and consistency to your co-parenting journey.

While it's not legally binding, a parenting plan serves as a reference point and can prevent unnecessary arguments or misunderstandings by setting clear expectations. It encourages both parents to work together in creating a nurturing and supportive environment for their child.

While parenting plans are not legal documents, courts often view them favourably. This is because a plan demonstrates that both parents are committed to working together for the child's best interests. If disputes escalate to legal proceedings, a well-drafted plan can show the court that you've already made efforts to collaborate, which may influence their decisions.

What to include in a parenting plan

Every parenting plan is unique, shaped by the needs of the child, the capacity of each parent and the dynamics of their relationship post-separation. When approached with cooperation and intention, these plans can create a stable, nurturing foundation that allows a child to thrive. Here are some of the key areas to consider when drafting or revisiting your parenting plan:

- **Living arrangements:** Clarify where the child will primarily live and outline a consistent visitation schedule. This may include regular weekdays, weekends and overnight stays. Be realistic and child-centred. Think about travel time, schooling and the importance of routine.
- **Communication between parents:** Decide on a primary method of communication (for example, text, email, co-parenting apps), and set boundaries around frequency and what topics are appropriate. Establishing expectations early helps avoid misunderstandings later.
- **Financial responsibilities:** Discuss how both day-to-day and unexpected expenses will be covered. Will there be a fixed monthly contribution, a shared bank account for child-related costs or reimbursement 'as needed'? Be transparent and revisit this regularly as circumstances change.
- **Holidays and special occasions:** Create a fair, thoughtful plan for school breaks, religious holidays, birthdays and other important events. You may choose to alternate years or even split the day, – whatever works best for your child's sense of inclusion and stability.
- **Introducing new partners:** Agree on when and how new relationships should be introduced to your child. A general rule, such as waiting until the relationship is established or notifying the other parent before any introduction, can avoid unnecessary confusion or tension.

Prevention is better than cure

I constantly encourage parents to be proactive rather than reactive. It's much easier to have calm and constructive conversations about your child's needs when things are stable rather than waiting until conflict arises. Many parents think, 'We don't need a parenting plan because everything is fine right now.' That's wonderful – until it's not.

Life is unpredictable and dynamics can shift. Disagreements, misunderstandings or events like new partners or financial changes can complicate co-parenting. Without a written plan, verbal agreements often fade into misinterpretations or selective memories intervene, leaving room for disputes. A parenting plan is your shelter before the storm, providing structure and security. It's a chance to map out how to handle all the critical aspects of raising your child together.

Remember, when emotions run high, it's much harder to make decisions that are fair and child-centred, but a parenting plan offers several benefits:

- **Clarity and consistency:** Both parents know what is expected of them, reducing misunderstandings.
- **A reference point:** When disagreements arise, you can refer back to the agreed-upon terms instead of debating past conversations.
- **A child-centred focus:** The plan ensures decisions are made with the child's best interests in mind, rather than being driven by emotions.

Having a well-structured parenting plan significantly increases the chances of successful co-parenting, especially when compared to situations where no formal plan exists.

Parents who are aligned, and operate from a shared understanding regarding routines, responsibilities and boundaries, tend to report higher levels of satisfaction and fewer conflicts. Research shows that children benefit directly from this stability. Where parents cooperate effectively, children demonstrate better emotional well-being, stronger relationships with both parents, and fewer behavioural issues.

A large-scale review by Dr Linda Nielsen found that children raised in cooperative shared parenting arrangements consistently fared better across 90% of the outcomes studied, including:

- Mental health
- Academic achievement
- Family relationships

The key factor wasn't just time spent with each parent, but the level of cooperation between them. In contrast, children exposed to ongoing conflict, instability or unresolved disputes between parents were more likely to experience emotional stress, behavioural challenges and strained family bonds. This highlights how crucial cooperation, not just custody arrangements, is to a child's long-term well-being.

If tensions are high or productive conversations seem impossible, mediation can be a powerful tool. Mediation is where a neutral third party helps parents move from emotional reactions to constructive decisions. Mediation shifts the focus from 'winning' to what's genuinely best for your child. While mediators cannot offer legal advice and must remain professionally neutral, their benefit comes in often diffusing conflict and creating a safer space for decision-making to occur.

Practical tips for parenting plan success

Experienced child protection lawyer Nieki Shaw, who runs the social media platform @LegallyNik, advises that a parenting plan works best when it is approached as a living, child-focused framework rather than a rigid rulebook. The aim is not perfection, but clarity, consistency and reducing conflict for your child. Here's how:

- **Start with an open mind and a willingness to compromise:** You don't need to agree on everything, but you do need to agree that your child's well-being comes first.
- **Create a parenting plan as early as possible:** Even a simple interim plan can provide structure and reduce uncertainty during an emotionally charged period. It can always be refined later.
- **Be thoughtful about how the plan is made:** Some parents work well drafting it together. Others find it more effective for one parent to prepare a draft for the other to review and amend. Where communication is difficult, mediation or a neutral professional can help keep the focus on the child.
- **Use templates where helpful:** There are many parenting plan templates available online that cover practical issues such as routines, holidays, handovers, communication and decision-making. These can

be a useful starting point and adapted to suit your family's needs. The Children and Family Court Advisory and Support Service (Cafcass) has produced one, for example. Things to consider are:

- **Avoid revisiting past grievances:** A parenting plan is not about what went wrong between you; it is about what your child needs moving forward.
- **Keep it flexible:** Children grow, and their emotional, educational and social needs change. Build in space to review and update the plan as needed.
- **See it from your child's perspective:** They are the ones moving between households and adjusting to two environments. Cooperation between parents can make that transition feel safe rather than stressful.
- **Document agreements clearly:** Verbal agreements can easily be misunderstood or forgotten. Write everything down and consider using a co-parenting app to keep arrangements, messages and calendars in one place
- **Don't be afraid to ask for support:** Whether through mediation, family therapy, support services or professional advice, seeking help is a strength and often protects children from ongoing conflict.

A strong parenting plan isn't rigid, it's reliable. It doesn't demand perfection, but it does require effort, empathy and a shared commitment to your child's peace of mind.

Making your agreement legally binding

If you and your co-parent would like to establish your parenting agreement as a legally binding document, you might consider involving a legal advisor to draft it into a consent order. This is a legal document that formally confirms your agreement and can be approved by a court, giving it enforceable authority. It gives both parents peace of mind, ensuring that the agreed arrangements are not only clear but also protected by law.

While a consent order provides legal backing, this process should not be used to control or punish the other parent, but rather as a tool to promote clarity, stability and fairness for everyone involved, most importantly, the child. Note that once a consent order is in place, making amendments often requires returning to court, so flexibility and future considerations should be factored into the drafting process.

When one parent won't cooperate

Creating any type of plan requires cooperation, but I recognise that not all parents are willing participants. For those of you struggling to communicate with an uncooperative co-parent, take the opportunity to think about the issues yourself. Even if you can't finalise the plan together immediately, putting your ideas down can provide a starting point for future discussions. Here are some practical steps if your co-parent refuses to engage:

- **Write a solo draft:** Create a parenting plan on your own. Outline what you believe is fair and child-centred. This becomes your reference and proposal when discussions do open.
- **Send an invitation, not a demand:** Share your draft with your co-parent by sending a calm message like, 'I've started putting together a parenting plan, because I want us both to have clarity moving forward. You're welcome to review and add your thoughts when you're ready.'
- **Use a communication app:** Tools like OurFamilyWizard or TalkingParents log all messages and can help reduce emotional communication. These tools often show the court your efforts to stay cooperative.
- **Stay consistent:** If your co-parent constantly changes plans or cancels contact, document everything. Keep records of agreed-upon arrangements and deviations. Courts look favourably on the parent showing consistency and child-centred intent.

- **Don't retaliate:** It's easy to want to match energy or fight fire with fire (*see* pp. 160–161), but your child benefits when you rise above conflict. Being the 'bigger person' isn't weak, it's wise. It protects your child's peace.

A parenting plan is a reminder of your focus – a reminder of what's important not just for your co-parent but for you. It's something you can review and reflect on to see if it's working in the way you hoped it would or if you've deviated from it yourself.

You don't need a willing co-parent to start creating structure. You just need clarity about what your child needs, what you can offer and what boundaries you're willing to set. Even if the other parent isn't consistent, you can be. Even if things feel messy, you can create peace.

However, if your co-parent actively sabotages agreements or uses the child to control situations, it may be time to speak to a legal advisor or family mediator. Even then, your parenting plan draft can serve as a foundation to work from. Plans may change and will often be tested, but the act of making one is a sign that you're committed to more than just reacting – you're committed to parenting with intention.

#21

Custody arrangements

Co-parenting is more common now than ever, with a growing number of households headed by a single parent. In today's modern family structure, child custody arrangements play a crucial role in providing stability and support for children, even amid the challenges of separation.

These arrangements have become an integral part of everyday life, helping a child feel secure as they navigate life between two homes. While some of you as parents may feel confident in your current set-up, others may struggle to know where to start or what options are most appropriate for their family.

When it comes to co-parenting arrangements, flexibility and understanding your child's unique needs are essential. Just as no two children are alike, the same goes for co-parenting approaches. It's about finding the method that best suits your child by considering a range of factors, such as:

- The age of the child
- Each parent's ability to care for them
- The child's attachment to both parents
- The living situations of each parent
- Any history of abuse or neglect, if applicable
- The child's preferences, based on age

Let's explore some of the most common custody arrangements and consider how each might serve different family dynamics.

Sole residency

In this arrangement, the child lives primarily with one parent, while the other parent may have visitation rights, either through a court agreement or mutual arrangement. This could include overnight stays or simply regular visits.

Some of the pros are:

- **Stability:** Provides consistency, especially for younger children, as they have a single home base.
- **Emotional security:** Some children thrive with a primary caregiver, particularly if they are very young or strongly attached to one parent.
- **Simplicity:** Fewer transitions between homes can reduce confusion or stress for the child.

Some of the cons are:

- **Limited relationship with non-resident parent:** The non-resident parent may miss key moments, potentially weakening their bond with the child.
- **Parental imbalance:** The primary parent bears the brunt of the daily responsibilities, which can lead to burnout.
- **Emotional impact:** The child may feel disconnected from the non-resident parent, leading to feelings of abandonment or emotional distance.

Joint residency

In this arrangement a child spends time living with both parents, who share parental responsibilities. While this might not always be on a 50/50 split, it's a more balanced approach.

Some of the pros are:

- **Balanced time:** Children can maintain a strong relationship with both parents, benefitting from shared experiences in each household.
- **Parental involvement:** Both parents have the opportunity to be actively involved in the child's life, from school events to everyday routines.
- **Reduced parental stress:** The parenting load is split, which can ease the burden on each individual parent.

Some of the cons are:

- **Potential instability:** Frequent moves between homes can be challenging for younger children or those with special needs, causing emotional or logistical stress.
- **Complex scheduling:** Managing school, activities and social lives across two homes can become complicated.
- **Differing parenting styles:** Inconsistent rules or routines between households can confuse or frustrate the child.

Non 50/50 split

In many cases, parents don't divide their time with the child equally. Popular schedules include alternating weekends with mid-week visits or extended weekends to allow the child more time with the non-resident parent.

Another option is a biweekly schedule, where the child spends one week with each parent. This can work well for older children with more structured routines or when parents live further apart.

Bird's nest parenting

This arrangement keeps the child in the family home, while the parents alternate living there. The parents will live elsewhere when it's not their time with the child. Although this arrangement often ends when the child leaves home, it can offer stability during childhood.

Some of the pros are:

- **Stability for the child:** The child remains in the family home, which provides a sense of security and consistency.
- **Less disruption:** The child doesn't have to adjust to different environments, making their day-to-day life more predictable.
- **Equal access:** Both parents continue to be a part of the child's life without the child feeling torn between two homes.

Some of the cons are:

- **Logistical strain on parents:** Moving between homes can be tiring and difficult for parents, especially if they live far from the family home.
- **Cost:** Maintaining a shared family home in addition to two separate residences can be financially burdensome.
- **Emotional complexity:** Parents may find it emotionally challenging to return to the family home, especially if the separation is still fresh or conflict is unresolved.

Flexible arrangements

This is when parents adjust the schedule week by week depending on work, school or other circumstances. It requires high levels of communication and cooperation between parents, but it allows the child to benefit from spending time with each parent when it suits both households.

Some of the pros are:

- **Adaptability:** Parents can adjust the schedule to accommodate work, school and social commitments, which can reduce stress for both parents and the child.

- **Responsive to the child's needs:** A flexible arrangement allows for changes based on the child's emotional or physical health, ensuring that they receive the best care at any given time.
- **Opportunity for cooperation:** Parents who communicate well can make decisions that benefit everyone, fostering a spirit of teamwork.

Some of the cons are:

- **Inconsistency:** A lack of structure may cause confusion or insecurity for the child, who might not know what to expect from week to week.
- **Requires high communication levels:** This arrangement demands constant coordination and communication between co-parents, which can be difficult if there are underlying tensions.
- **Potential imbalance:** If one parent is more flexible than the other, this arrangement may lead to one parent bearing more of the load, creating feelings of inequality.

Tailoring your co-parenting approach

Co-parenting arrangements are not static, whatever you choose. They need to evolve as children grow and their needs change. The best arrangement for your child today may not be the one that works a year from now. What works for a toddler may not be ideal for a school-aged child, and what suits a younger child may need to be adjusted as they transition into their teenage years.

This is why it's crucial to remain flexible and to be open when it comes to reassessing your arrangement. The key to a successful co-parenting arrangement is always to put the child's needs first, even though this may require both parents to set aside personal differences and focus on what is in the best interest of the family.

It's essential to observe how your child is responding to the current arrangement and be willing to have open discussions with your co-parent and child (dependent on age) if it seems that a change is needed. Rather than viewing your custody arrangement as a strict limit on the time you spend with your child, think of it as a baseline.

For instance, I often view my scheduled time with my child as the minimum I will spend with him, not the maximum. I make a conscious effort to find additional opportunities to spend quality time together, whether that's picking him up from school or planning extra outings. Of course, I always make sure to clear these additional plans with his mum first, to maintain open communication.

Just like you might work extra hours for financial gain, think of your parenting time as having the potential for 'overtime', but instead of financial benefit it's for the invaluable bonding experience with your child and to give the other parent a well-deserved break.

At the heart of this approach is flexibility and communication. It's about maintaining a routine that prioritises your child's well-being, ensuring that they feel secure, supported and loved at every stage of their development.

From the child's perspective

When I was reflecting on this, I felt it was important to tap into my own children's views, to better understand their feelings on custody arrangements. I asked my then 10-year-old son, 'How would you feel about living with me full-time or splitting time 50/50?' This would be a drastic increase in time spent together than the current routine. He paused, clearly uncomfortable, so I reassured him that it was just a hypothetical question. He didn't need to answer, but from his body language it was clear that the idea didn't sit well with him. He wouldn't be too keen on it.

Does this mean I'm a bad parent? No. Does this mean he loves me less? No. What it means is that he's content with how things are now. He feels secure and loved in both homes, and his mum is doing an amazing job as well.

Upon reflection, why would he be happy living with me for extended periods? He has a great relationship with his mum, his friends all live near his mum's house, his brother and sister live there, his school is only a few minutes away, not to mention his stepdad, whom he loves being around, and is there as well. All these things make his mum's home the primary source of comfort and stability for him.

As co-parents, it's easy to get caught up in the idea of splitting time 50/50 or even trying to 'win' with custody arrangements. However, we often forget to stop and consider what our child truly wants. Despite any differences between parents, children don't see the issues. They just see two people they love. All they want is stability and comfort in both of their homes. This serves as a reminder that co-parenting isn't about winning or adhering to a rigid schedule, it's about adapting and responding to what's best for the child.

#22

Organising schedules

One of the most challenging aspects of co-parenting is coordinating schedules. You are two individuals with different work commitments, routines, extracurricular activities and responsibilities, yet you share the same child.

To be on a page that benefits your child you must be willing to commit to the juggling act of effective co-parenting, because consistency and predictability are crucial. Your child needs to know when and where they will be, who will be there and that they are loved by both parents, regardless of the logistics.

When it comes to milestones or special events we usually know about them well in advance, yet despite this awareness, some of us leave things until the last minute. We wait to book annual leave only to be told it's unavailable, or we rely on the other parent to remind us only to realise we've already made other plans on the required date.

This is an 'us' issue, not a 'them' issue. If we as parents do not take the time to write dates down, plan ahead and organise ourselves and our schedules, how can we expect to provide the consistency and reliability our child needs to feel safe and secure? Children thrive on routine and predictability, and the smallest act of preparation, from pencilling in a school performance, to requesting the day off work creates a sense of stability that reassures them.

Some of us remember every detail about friends' birthdays, our partner's anniversaries or a football match, yet we may overlook the school term dates, parent evenings, plays or concerts our child is performing in, sports days or a weekend trip our child is excited about.

Every missed opportunity to organise or prepare sends subtle messages to our child: that their important moments are negotiable, that uncertainty is normal or that their priorities are secondary.

Practical steps

When we plan ahead we show our child that their experiences matter, that they can trust us to be present and that their joy is our priority. The more effort we put into preparation, the more comfort, confidence and emotional stability we provide, allowing our child to focus on enjoying the moment, rather than worrying about what will or won't happen. There are several things you can do to make sure this happens:

Plan well in advance
Identify major events at the start of the year and request leave from work early to avoid last-minute conflicts.

Communicate clearly and consistently
Send reminders for upcoming events with dates, times and any responsibilities. Confirm pick-up and drop-off times in writing to avoid miscommunication.

Keep records
Document agreed arrangements, changes and confirmations. If disputes arise, this record-keeping can help resolve them calmly.

Use a shared calendar
Keep a digital calendar shared with your co-parent (try Google Calendar or a co-parenting app) to log all school events, extracurricular activities and family commitments.

Build flexibility into the routine
Life happens and not every plan will run perfectly. If possible, ensure there's a back-up plan for unexpected cancellations or delays, so your child's routine is preserved.

REFLECTION: HOW ORGANISED ARE YOU?

Use these questions to reflect on your current planning and scheduling habits:

- Am I proactively marking my child's important events in my calendar?
- Have I requested leave or made arrangements to be present for key moments?
- Do I communicate clearly and in advance with my co-parent?
- Do I have a system in place to manage unexpected changes while protecting my child's routine?

Special occasions

I write this with Christmas approaching, knowing that this year my kids will wake up with me. How do I know this? Because this has been our routine for much of our co-parenting journey.

Omari has grown used to this pattern over the years. One year, I collect him on Christmas Eve and take him back to his mum around 5 p.m. on Christmas Day. The next year, I collect him at 5 p.m. on Christmas Day and have him until Boxing Day, or whatever arrangement is agreed upon. The focus is always the same: ensuring that Christmas Day itself is a special, shared experience. It's a blessing that his mum was willing to work together, as having this routine in place allows for Omari to look forward to Christmas each year without the uncertainty of how the day might unfold. It allows him to be fully present, enjoying the moment with the comfort of knowing that no matter what, the routine remains consistent.

When Tyler came along and I began co-parenting with his mum, she was willing to fall into the same routine. Her generosity meant that both my boys could experience Christmas together, a moment that went beyond just her family. She understood the importance of Tyler sharing these moments with his brother. That was an incredibly beautiful act.

I am certain that this was not easy for her. Christmas is a significant event, full of family traditions and expectations. Yet she placed her wants and desires second to the needs of her child. That kind of selflessness is rare and it is a powerful example of prioritising what truly matters: the child's happiness.

This same energy and focus extends beyond Christmas to birthdays, family events, school trips and countless other occasions. There are many times I will adjust my schedule, swap dates or even double up on days to ensure Tyler does not miss out. Cousins' birthdays, school events, special occasions with his mum and her family – my role is not to control these moments, but to protect and amplify his joy.

I understand that some parents feel strongly about holding on to special occasions for themselves, refusing to allow the other parent to share in them, especially if they feel the other parent hasn't 'earned' it. I am not saying your feelings are wrong, but I will say this: your emotions cannot lead your decisions. Dislike for the other parent must never outweigh the love you have for your child. Your child's happiness and experiences must come first.

Special occasions also tend to be the moments when absent or inconsistent parents reappear, asking, or even demanding, time with their child. To those parents: your child is not just for Christmas or birthdays; they are for a lifetime. Your role is not seasonal; it is ongoing and requires dedication every day of the year. If you are unwilling to show up consistently, then you cannot fault the parent who has been there 24/7, 365 days a year, for saying no during these moments.

Being present every day earns the trust and opportunity to participate fully in these special occasions. Your child deserves your commitment not just on the calendar, but in the moments that matter most to them, throughout their entire childhood.

And to those primary parents who find themselves dealing with a reappearing co-parent around Christmas or other special occasions, I will never encourage you to block contact unless you genuinely believe your child's well-being is at risk. At the same time, I will never make you feel guilty for refusing last-minute requests or demands. You have been there and carried the responsibility with little to no support, help or even consideration from the other parent.

You have every right to feel angry, annoyed and frustrated – those emotions are valid. What I would ask, though, is that those emotions don't become the driving force behind your decision-making. Acknowledge how you feel, but try not to let those feelings alone determine the choices you make for your child.

The following exercise isn't about shame or guilt, it's a chance to reflect on where your focus may have shifted and how you can redirect it to put your child's well-being at the heart of every decision. Being honest with your responses creates space for growth and improvement.

REFLECTION: SCHEDULING SELF-ANALYSIS

Use these questions to evaluate how your scheduling for special occasions is impacting your child:

- Do I prioritise my child's experience over my own convenience or preferences?
- Have I communicated clearly with my co-parent about upcoming events?
- Am I flexible when necessary, while still maintaining consistency for my child?
- Do my child's birthdays, holidays and milestones allow them to feel loved by both parents?
- Are there ways I can improve planning to reduce stress for my child?

#23

Pick-ups and drop-offs

Although we're talking about a child and not a parcel, pick-ups and drop-offs truly don't need to be as emotional or chaotic as they often become. If we strip away ego, resentment and assumptions, this part of co-parenting can be one of the simplest things we do. Think about how an Amazon delivery works. A driver arrives, hands over the parcel and leaves. If you're returning something, you package it up, take it to a drop-off point, hand it over and it's done. There's no argument, no hostility, no power struggles... Why? Because everyone understands their role and focuses solely on the task.

That's exactly how transitions between homes should feel for a child: calm, predictable, respectful and centred on their well-being. It should be two adults, aware of the agreed time, location and what's needed, doing exactly what's necessary to ensure the child moves between homes with ease, comfort and reassurance. But here's where things often go wrong, and where the child pays the biggest price:

- Lateness that leaves a child waiting with their bag packed, feeling unimportant
- No-shows that deflate their excitement and trust
- Forgotten items – school bags, medication, uniforms – that place unnecessary stress on the child, not just the parents
- Last-minute changes that create unpredictability, anxiety and confusion
- Conflict at the door, raised voices, passive aggression or attempts to intimidate.

None of these moments only impact the parents. They leave the child feeling caught in the middle, responsible or unsafe, and that is the kind of damage we should be avoiding at all costs.

As I've said, during the height of conflict between me and my son's mum, she asked for pick-ups to happen at his grandma's. Was it frustrating? Yes! Especially when I had to drive past her home to get there. But I still did it, because the goal was simple: to see my child, not my co-parent.

If something as reasonable as a neutral location, a contact centre or a middle person stops you from seeing your child, then the real question becomes: do you want time with your child or are you more interested in seeing, controlling or confronting the other parent?

Pick-ups and drop-offs will never be perfect. Life happens. Delays happen, but the foundation should always be the same: respect the schedule, respect each other and above all protect the child's emotional safety, every single time. There aren't many occasions when I speak in absolutes, but this is one of them:

- Do NOT speak negatively about the other parent in front of the child.
- Do NOT argue in front of the child.
- And NEVER place the child in the middle of you, mentally or physically.

You are always in control of your own behaviour. How you speak, how you react and how you choose to handle tense moments is never determined by the other parent. So if you ever feel triggered, unsafe or overwhelmed, remove yourself from the situation calmly and responsibly.

Your child is not a referee, a messenger or a rope in your tug-of-war. They are a young person trying to understand themselves, their world and where they belong. That alone is enough for them to carry. Don't add your conflict on top of that.

Let your child see your example. Even if the other parent is behaving disrespectfully, you don't have to respond in the same way. A fire only grows when it's given oxygen, so the moment you retaliate, you feed it, you strengthen it, and now your child becomes surrounded by the flames of adult conflict. Show your child what safe, controlled, respectful behaviour looks like, even when it's difficult.

Tips for a successful, child-focused handover

Not every parent is working with a cooperative co-parent, and that's a reality many face. But if you are genuinely committed to putting your child first, these steps can drastically reduce conflict and create a calmer, more predictable experience for your child:

Plan the handover time in advance

Planning isn't just about convenience for you as adults; it protects your child's emotional security. A consistent routine helps children feel safe, reduces anxiety and stops them from wondering what's happening every week.

Instead of texting a few hours before, agree on a clear routine, such as collecting your child every other Friday evening at 7 p.m. and returning them on Sunday afternoon. This won't work for everyone, depending on work schedules or activities, but the goal is to find something that works for all parties, not just one parent. Once a routine exists, stick to it. This also reduces the need for constant communication, because everyone knows the plan.

You don't message your boss every week to confirm your shift–you only contact them if something changes, and you do so early because you understand the consequences. When it comes to your child, the consequence of poor planning is their mental and emotional well-being.

Agree on what each home provides

Every family does this differently and that's okay, because what matters is clarity. In my situation, Tyler usually brings a bag when he comes to mine. That's because most of his clothes and toys are at his mum's house, and anything I buy him I buy knowing it will stay there. I do this because I want him to get the most enjoyment and wear out of these items. This works for us because we've discussed and agreed on it.

If you have a 50/50 arrangement, it's usually more beneficial to have both homes fully equipped so the child isn't constantly transporting essentials.

There shouldn't be an expectation that the primary parent provides everything, but there should always be a conversation. Avoid assumptions, because they're one of the biggest causes of unnecessary arguments.

Have the child ready on time

A child who has been sitting by the door waiting often feels anxious or disappointed if the parent is late. Likewise, a child who is rushed out of the door in a panic, because the parent wasn't prepared, absorbs that stress. Everyone should already know the agreed time, so preparation should be simple.

Although we have an agreed time, I still usually call Tyler or his mum when I'm 10 minutes away. It gives him time to put on his coat and trainers, so that when I arrive he's ready to go without any pressure, waiting or frustration. This small step prevents unnecessary conflict, avoids waiting on doorsteps and keeps the transition smooth for the child.

Understand boundaries around entering the home

No parent is automatically entitled to walk into the other parent's home. A handover is just that – a handover. The child leaves one home and goes to the other.

If the relationship allows for a parent to step inside, that can be lovely for the child. There have been times when I've popped into Tyler's mum's home for a minute and he's loved showing me new toys or seeing me interact positively with his mum and stepdad.

Moments like that can give a child a powerful sense of peace, but I never expect to be invited in and will stay outside unless welcomed in. This shows respect for their home, their boundaries and, most importantly, it models healthy behaviour for the child.

Pick-ups and drop-offs are an opportunity

For some of you, these handover moments may be the closest your child gets to seeing both parents in the same space. That's why it's so important that these moments model safety, peace and care, showing your child that adults can create a calm and loving environment, even during transitions. These experiences will either become something your child appreciates and remembers positively as they grow, or something they dread.

REFLECTION: HOW DOES YOUR CHILD SEE HANDOVERS?

Take your time with each question below, and be honest.

- If my child described handovers in one sentence, what would they say?
- What example do I want to set for my child, even if my co-parent behaves poorly?
- How consistently do I follow the agreed plan, time and boundaries?
- What boundaries do I need to protect my own peace, so I can show up better?
- What is one promise I can make to myself today for the sake of my child's emotional safety?

#24

School days

According to the Education Endowment Foundation (EEF), effective parental engagement can lead to learning gains of approximately three months over the course of a year, while a study by an academic called John Hattie found that parental engagement throughout the school years could be equivalent to adding two or three years to that child's education overall. This research is a profound reminder that when parents show up consistently, take an interest and reinforce learning at home, they are effectively extending their child's academic journey far beyond the classroom.

Now although these findings highlight a critical truth – that the involvement of parents, both parents, matters deeply and measurably – even when one parent is less involved, the consistent engagement, encouragement and support from the other parent can still have a powerful impact. In other words, your dedication alone helps your child feel supported, secure and motivated to learn.

Education is one of the most stable and consistent environments in a child's life. It offers routine, structure and a sense of progression through defined milestones. But it's more than just a place to gain knowledge – it's where children begin to shape their identity, form relationships and develop self-worth. When both parents engage with this environment, whether through helping with homework, attending school events or simply showing an interest in their child's day, they reinforce the message that learning matters and that their child matters.

In situations where co-parents struggle to get along or communicate, school can serve as a neutral space and shared priority. No matter how strained the relationship may be, I would hope that both parents agree on the importance of their child's education. Therefore, the power of shared educational involvement can be a unifying force.

It sends a strong message to the child: we may not be together, but we are together for you. That message can be transformative, so think of parental involvement not just as support, but as an investment. Consistent engagement has the power to transform your child's experience of school and their outcomes.

As I write this chapter, I've just received an email from my son's school about his upcoming parents' evening. Normally, I'd wait for a message from his mum as she's always been proactive in moments like this, but this time I decide to take the initiative. I message her first, offering my availability and asking what works best for her.

It's a small shift, but it matters. This moment of shared coordination wouldn't be possible if I wasn't included on the school's email list. Without that access, I'd still be relying on her for every update, placing the full weight of communication and organisation on her shoulders. That's not fair and it's not sustainable. Being informed directly allows me to be proactive, not reactive. It takes pressure off her, shows my son we are both involved and strengthens our co-parenting dynamic.

Your child's school experience should be something you are both actively involved in, not just when it comes to celebrating good grades or graduations. It's not enough to show up for the highlights reel; you need to be there for the everyday challenges and growth, too.

The education system recognises all parents as having the right to be involved in their child's schooling. This means both parents can and should receive information about their child's progress, records and educational experience.

For day-to-day purposes, the school will typically communicate with the parent with whom the child lives during the school week. However, it's unfair and unsustainable to expect the primary parent to manage this alone and ensure they pass on every bit of information to the other parent. That's extra work they don't need to carry. Simply contacting the school to ensure you're added to their database will:

- Take pressure off the primary parent
- Ensure you stay up to date with your child's progress
- Show your child that both parents care equally about their education.

I get constant emails from my child's school. Some I don't need, but others are invaluable. Sometimes, I catch things my child's mum might have missed. Two heads really are better than one when it comes to supporting your child's education.

It's the same story when it comes to homework. I remember Tyler getting his first detention, because he didn't submit his homework on time. When I asked him why, it was like he was speaking a secret language only a kid could understand. His reasons didn't make any sense. Simply put, he forgot.

When I found out about the detention, my first instinct could have been, 'Why didn't his mum make sure he did his homework?' But the truth is, she could easily say the exact same thing to me, as we are both his parents, and I'd have to admit, 'I didn't even know he had homework.' At that point, the blame game doesn't help us help Tyler.

The truth is, Tyler is 11 now and needs to take responsibility for his own actions. Homework is his responsibility, not ours. But as his parent, it's my responsibility to guide and support him, and I can't do that effectively if I'm not kept in the loop. That important information can come from the school system or by me actively engaging with Tyler myself. It's not fair or realistic to expect his mum to act like my personal assistant, constantly updating me.

Give them their memories

In the UK, primary school ends at Year 6, when a child is around 11 years old, although this transition may occur at different stages globally. What comes next isn't just a new school, it's a new world. Secondary school marks a profound shift, not only in education, but in your child's sense of self, their environment and even how they relate to you. Suddenly, they're surrounded by older children, navigating independence and often grappling with pressure you can no longer shield them from. It's as if you watch their innocence quietly slip away.

Gone are the days of Father Christmas letters, handmade gifts for Mother's Day or Father's Day, tea parties with parents in the classroom and the magic of nativity plays. The egg and spoon races, parents cheering from the sidelines and your child reaching for your hand at the school gate all slowly fade.

It goes from them holding your hand tightly, hesitating as they walk through those gates for the very first time… To one day asking if they can make their own way to school, because they no longer see a need for you to be there. It's a subtle shift at first, a growing independence, but it's also a reminder that your presence, once essential and unquestioned, becomes optional in their eyes.

I don't say this to make you sad, but to remind you: these moments don't last forever. And once they're gone, they're gone. I often find myself looking at photos from when my boys were in primary school and I wonder where that time went. One day you're signing permission slips for class trips and the next you're helping them register for college.

These moments belong to both you and your co-parent, to remember, to enjoy, to be proud of, but they're ultimately for your child. You've had your time. Your firsts and lasts. Your assemblies and school plays. Let them have theirs without guilt, confusion or tension. Don't let their memories be laced with anxiety over which parent came and which didn't. Don't allow your relationship with each other to cast a shadow over school plays, parents' evenings or pick-up time. These are the little moments that shape how safe, supported and seen a child feels.

And when the school sends out those optional notices for school photos, special events or trip sign-ups, some resident parents may think they're not obligated to share this. And they're right, it's not required, but co-parenting isn't about doing the bare minimum, it's about showing up for your child even when it's inconvenient. It's about thinking, 'How would I feel if I missed out on that photo or that milestone?'

If you want your co-parent to cooperate, show them what cooperation looks like. Even when they haven't done it before, even when they might not do the same. Do it so your child doesn't have to carry the weight of your separation. Do it so you're never the reason the other parent didn't show up.

Yes, maybe they never used to bother. Maybe they still won't. But when you share the information, you shift the focus. The responsibility lies where it should: with the parent who chooses not to engage, not with the one who kept it to themselves.

You remove their excuse and, more importantly, you protect your child's chance to feel supported by both parents. Because in the end, school isn't about you. It's their experience. Don't let your silence or stubbornness be the reason they remember it differently.

Negotiating the school system

Navigating your child's school life as co-parents can be challenging, especially when emotions are still raw or routines are shifting. But this phase is crucial, not just for your child's academic progress, but for their sense of stability and support.

The following list isn't about getting everything perfect. It's here to guide you through this period, helping to keep your child's best interests at the centre of every decision you make when it comes to their education and school environment. Here are some things to consider:

- Talking to school administrators to establish plans for them to share all relevant information with both parents
- Remaining or becoming actively involved in your child's education, even after separation
- Informing the school if you and the other parent are divorced or separated, and if the child spends time in both homes
- Staying engaged with your child about school: homework, tests, friendships, challenges and what excites them
- Attending school events whenever possible. If possible, sit with your co-parent and show your child that their education unites you both. If not, ensure there is no negative energy felt within this space, as your child may pick this up
- Talking to your co-parent about any concerns you notice in your child's physical, emotional, mental or behavioural well-being. Working together is always better than handling it alone
- Discussing school-related expenses: who pays what, how costs will be shared and how unexpected expenses will be communicated and covered.

And here are some things to try to avoid:

- Your child being the go-between for school updates and information. That's not their responsibility
- Assuming the other parent will handle everything, especially if they took the lead on school matters while you were together. It's time to step up
- Ignoring emails or communication from the school just because you weren't the 'main contact' before
- Treating school involvement as optional or only for special occasions. Every parent needs to play an active role, all year long
- Making your child feel like they must choose which parent to involve or keep informed. School belongs to them, not to either of you alone.

Checklist for co-parenting through school

Use the checklist below to reflect on your current engagement and identify areas where you can make improvements:

Communication and involvement

- Am I listed as a contact with my child's school?
- Do I receive school emails, newsletters and updates directly?
- Do I regularly communicate with my co-parent about school-related matters?
- Do I know who my child's teachers are?

Homework and daily support

- Do I ask my child about their homework or school day?
- Am I aware of upcoming assignments, tests or projects?
- Do I help my child manage their school responsibilities without blaming the other parent?

Collaboration as parents

- Have we agreed on how to split or manage school-related expenses?
- Do we have a shared system (calendar, app or notes) for important school dates?
- Have we talked about our child's emotional or academic struggles as a team?

School presence

- Have I attended school events this term?
- Have I sat with or communicated amicably with my co-parent at these events?
- Do I help create an environment where our child sees both parents equally involved?

School holidays

- Have we discussed how holidays will be split this year?
- Do we take into account our child's wants and needs, not just our convenience?
- Have we agreed on plans early to avoid last-minute stress or confusion?

#25

What happens in the holidays?

Before we take a deeper look at school holidays, it's important to note that circumstances and routine will always vary from household to household. Some families may have relatives who can help look after the child, meaning less back-and-forth between parents. One parent might have a more flexible work schedule or more annual leave, so each situation will be unique. However, what's crucial to understand is that no one parent should bear the full burden of managing everything alone, and the focus should always be on what's best for your child. It's not just about logistics, it's about creating an environment where both parents, no matter the circumstances, are actively willing to show up for their child.

Growing up, I remember spending school holidays at my nan's house and occasionally, when it was affordable, I would go to a youth club nearby, Sir Phillips Game Centre, which became close to my heart. It was there I made great friends of all ages (shout out to Wesley and Ashley). The club offered me a place to have fun instead of being stuck indoors watching TV or playing the same games over and over again.

When I was old enough to be on my own, the financial pressure on Mum eased and I spent time with my friends around the estate, playing games like forty-forty or heading down to the park with the boys (Shaun, Courtney, Leon and TJ) to play football for hours on end. Now, although I was old enough to occupy myself for most of the day, Mum still had to make sure there was money for necessities before she could head to work.

The reason I'm sharing this is to highlight the difference in roles. My dad played no part in these decisions. He wasn't concerned about what his son was doing during the holidays, nor was he under the financial pressures my mum was. There were moments when it must have felt like Mum was working just to pay for me to go to clubs or to eat.

Reflecting on this as a man, I feel both overwhelmed with gratitude and frustration, because that was never how it should have been. One parent should never have to shoulder the weight of raising a child alone, especially when the other parent is absent, physically and emotionally.

In many countries, the dates of school holidays are known well in advance. In the UK, for example, schools typically provide term dates a year ahead, allowing co-parents to be proactive and have discussions on how best to navigate these breaks. I always reach out to my child's mum and ask, 'What works best for you and lil man?' Because no matter how much I love my son, I know he might not always want to spend the whole holiday with me.

There may be opportunities for him to see his cousins, spend time with Grandma or do fun activities with his mum. So, I arrange activities for us to enjoy together and offer him the option to stay with me during the holidays, giving both him and his mum the flexibility to make the most of the time.

School holiday challenges

Recently, I asked my audience what their biggest struggles are when it comes to school holidays and I was overwhelmed by the number of responses. I want to share some of them here, not just to remind you that you're not alone, but to offer practical solutions, support and space for reflection.

School holidays can shine a light on the imbalance that already exists in many co-parenting set-ups. The emotional and logistical weight often falls on one parent, usually the one with primary care, and this imbalance becomes especially hard to carry when the other parent isn't willing to share the load.

'My co-parent doesn't want to use their annual leave'

This was one of people's most common frustrations. In some cases, one parent ends up using all their annual leave to cover childcare, while the other feels free to use theirs for rest or holidays.

Annual leave is a right, not a luxury, but how it's used matters, especially if you're a parent or co-parent. Choosing not to use any of it to support your child during school holidays doesn't just leave the other parent under pressure, it places your child in a potentially unstable situation.

That said, not everyone has the same flexibility. Some jobs make taking time off difficult or financially risky. If that's the case, then communication and alternative solutions become even more important. If you're a parent who can't or won't take annual leave, consider this instead:

- **Speak to family members:** Is there a grandparent, aunt, uncle or trusted friend who can step in for a day or two? Helping coordinate childcare is still showing up for your child.
- **Offer additional financial support:** The cost of school holidays often increases significantly. If you can't give time, help cover the cost of holiday clubs, additional meals or activities that keep your child happy and cared for.

Work together to make a plan before the holiday starts. Whether that's alternating leave, combining resources or agreeing on financial support, the goal is to lighten the load and create consistency for your child. Don't focus on what you can't do; focus on what you can.

'I'm working full-time and trying to juggle childcare alone'

This is the emotional and physical toll many parents carry in silence, working full-time jobs while trying to ensure their child is safe, entertained and cared for during the long school breaks.

It's incredibly hard to focus on your job while worrying about who's looking after your child or how they're spending their day. The guilt is heavy and the exhaustion is real. You're doing the job of two people and often without recognition or rest.

While seeking my audiences' views on what they struggled with, I also asked what they found to be of help during these moments, because, as I reminded them, we focus on the solution, not the problem. Supportive solutions shared by other parents included:

- **Plan ahead as much as possible:** School holidays are known in advance, so build a rough plan to reduce stress closer to the time.
- **Use your community:** Connect with other parents in similar situations – you may be able to swap days, share pick-ups or take turns hosting playdates.
- **Explore free or low-cost holiday clubs:** Many councils, charities and community centres offer free kids' clubs or subsidised activities, especially during summer and half-term breaks.
- **Buy tickets early:** Planning days out in advance can help you secure cheaper prices and reduce last-minute decision fatigue.

While you may not always have practical support from your co-parent, lean into the networks that do exist. Be open to asking for help and remember, creating a village around your child isn't a sign of weakness, it's a sign of strength.

'Everything goes up during the holidays and no one talks about it'

Whether it's the rising cost of childcare, extra meals at home, days out or pressure to entertain, school holidays often bring significant financial strain. And when the financial support isn't shared equally, it leaves one parent feeling overwhelmed and isolated.

You're not imagining it. Many parents report not only higher spending during holidays, but also feeling frustrated when the other parent doesn't contribute or even acknowledge this extra burden.

If you're not the primary caregiver, offering extra financial support during the holidays isn't just helpful, it's necessary. Even a small contribution towards food, clubs or travel can make a huge difference. Money shouldn't be used as a form of control or punishment; it should be part of a shared effort to give your child the best experience possible. Smart suggestions from parents include:

- **Budget early:** Set aside small amounts monthly in preparation for the holidays.
- **Use tax-free childcare schemes or vouchers:** If they're available in your country, that is.
- **Team up with other parents:** Share costs for trips, babysitters or even food during joint playdates.

School holidays can be one of the clearest mirrors of imbalance in a co-parenting relationship, but they're also an opportunity to reset. The goal isn't perfection, it's partnership. Whether it's time, effort or finances, both parents have a role to play. Use this chapter as a reminder that you're not alone in how you feel, but also as motivation to shift the focus from frustration to forward-thinking.

#26

Child maintenance

It wouldn't surprise me if some of you have jumped straight to this chapter without having read anything previously. After all, child maintenance issues are among the most frequently asked questions I encounter.

From parents wondering if they should be receiving more, to those questioning if they should be paying additional amounts on top of what they already contribute, and even some of you who just want to vent about how manipulative your co-parent is when it comes to child maintenance - there are so many aspects to discuss and it's crucial to address these concerns thoroughly.

What is child maintenance?

Child maintenance is the financial support that the non-resident parent provides to the resident parent to contribute to their child's everyday living costs. These costs include essentials such as food, clothing, housing and education – everything that contributes to the child's well-being and development.

In the UK, when parents can't agree on child maintenance arrangements themselves, the Child Maintenance Service (CMS) may become involved if one or the other parent decides to contact them. The CMS calculates the amount given based on the paying parent's income, while considering factors like how many other children that parent has and how many nights a year the child stays with them.

Every country has its own system for managing child maintenance, but the core purpose is the same: to make sure children receive consistent financial support from both parents, regardless of their relationship status. Because laws differ from country to country, the best step for parents outside the UK is to check their local government or official child support agency. A simple search in your country for 'child support services' or 'child maintenance' will take you to the correct government site.

Weaponising what is owed

The aim of the UK's CMS – and the aim of similar organisations in other countries – is simple: to provide a fair and standardised approach to ensure children, not parents, receive the support they need. I emphasise 'children' here because many believe the money given is a favour to the primary parent. I'll admit, I used to think this way myself.

I remember when my son's mum and I first split up. We had no formal financial arrangement; I just paid what I felt like and bought what I thought was needed. At one point, we agreed on a set amount, but this often fluctuated depending on how I felt or if we'd recently argued. I'd delay payments or act like I didn't have the money.

You may ask why? Simply because controlling money was the only card I could use to get to my co-parent. I couldn't withhold the child as I wasn't the primary parent, but I could withhold money, or so I thought.

Then one day, I got a letter from the CMS, completely out of the blue. My son's mum hadn't warned me or told me this was happening – she simply decided enough was enough. And honestly ... good on her!

I don't blame her, or any parent, for doing this. Who did I think I was, trying to control finances based on how I felt? Using money as a way to hurt my co-parent and potentially my child? How could my child's mum, or any parent, plan their life, their bills or manage their responsibilities with someone acting so unpredictably?

When I found out, I was furious. I remember going to her with the classic line, 'You know by going to the CMS you might get less, right? So don't come asking me for anything else if that happens.' Her response has stuck with me ever since: 'I would rather get less each month and know what I'm getting, than have you control what I get based on how you feel.'

At the time I was still raging, but I couldn't argue with her logic. She was right. How can anyone plan their life when they have no idea what they'll be paid each month? Imagine your boss telling you they might pay you less this month or not at all – not because you had worked fewer hours, or had days off, but simply because they didn't feel like it. You'd be rushing straight to HR, wouldn't you?

Financial stability for your child

This experience taught me a crucial lesson: child maintenance isn't about giving money to your ex. It's about ensuring your child has the stability they need. It's not a bargaining chip or a way to assert control. It's an obligation – a responsibility you owe your child, to make sure their basic needs are met, no matter how you feel about the other parent.

When we argue over child maintenance, it's easy to get caught up in personal grievances and lose sight of what's important. It's not about the money or even about the co-parent – it's about the child. If you find yourself in a similar situation, take a moment to step back and ask yourself: is what I'm doing in the best interest of my child? Am I acting out of spite, or am I genuinely thinking about their well-being?

Child maintenance isn't a punishment. It's a responsibility. We may not always get along with our co-parent, but we must always prioritise our child's needs above all else. The truth is, the CMS exists because too many parents, me included, failed to see the importance of financial support and consistency.

Planning for your child's future can't be dictated by emotions, arguments or disagreements. It's dictated by what your child needs to thrive – predictability, stability and security. So, next time you feel tempted to use money as a weapon, remember who it's actually for.

In your control

In an ideal world there would be no need for a service such as CMS, but, as you know, this world is far from ideal. Now, unfortunately for some, in the UK, if you don't deal with the financial arrangements for your child yourself, this is the only service available.

The thing to note here, though, is that whether or not the CMS is involved will be determined by your own actions and whether you can come to the table as two adults to discuss matters such as your child's needs and well-being, and find a way to agree on an amount you both feel is reasonable.

Growing up, I saw the stress my mother faced as a single parent, covering every bill on her own because there was no financial contribution from my father. The CMS ensures that doesn't happen to others, by holding parents accountable for their child's financial needs, so personally I'm a fan of the CMS, because it provides clarity. Both I and my child's mother know exactly what to expect each month, which allows us to plan our lives more effectively.

However, the CMS isn't without its critics. Some parents feel it doesn't account for individual circumstances, such as paying parent's living expenses and other financial commitments; the time the child spends with each parent; and concerns that the money may not be used appropriately for the child's needs.

This has led to a perception that the CMS can be inflexible or unsympathetic to these concerns, but for now, in the UK, the CMS is the only option available unless you as adults come to an agreement between yourselves, which is something I would always encourage.

Calculating the cost

For those of you who are interested in understanding how much you should be paying or potentially receiving, head over to your equivalent service's website, which will be able to provide you with all the necessary information. You should also find an online calculator that will give you a rough estimate of what you should pay or receive.

There are some key differences in how the US equivalent of child maintenance, child support, is handled, when compared to the UK. While both countries consider the income of the paying parent, US states may also factor in the custodial parent's income, childcare costs and health insurance expenses.

The US often employs more aggressive enforcement tactics. These can include wage garnishment, interception of tax refunds, suspension of driver's or professional licences and even imprisonment for significant arrears. In the US, child support cases often involve court proceedings, whereas the UK's CMS aims to handle matters administratively, reducing the need for court involvement.

Despite these differences, both systems share the common goal of ensuring that children receive adequate financial support from both parents.

Part Three

Co-parenting with difficult people

#27

Managing conflict

Conflict in your co-parenting relationship is bound to occur. It's natural, because conflicts occur in any relationship. No matter how well-intentioned both parents may be, disagreements will arise, but how these disagreements are handled is often more important than the actual issue itself.

The 3 Cs

This is where the 3 Cs come in. They form a simple but powerful framework for managing conflict in co-parenting:

1. Calm
2. Child-focused
3. Compromise

It's a practical approach designed to help you navigate difficult conversations without losing sight of what matters most – your child's well-being. No matter how much you try, you will never be able to control your ex-partner's emotions, decisions or actions, but you can absolutely control your own.

1. C is for calm

Emotional regulation is your superpower.

Remaining calm is often easier said than done, especially if your co-parent is being difficult, unresponsive, controlling or manipulative. But calm is not weakness. It's control. It's choosing to respond instead of react. It's the ability to pause when provoked, to speak when ready and to disengage when things escalate unnecessarily.

Many co-parenting disputes spiral, not because of the issue at hand, but because calmness is lost in the heat of the moment. Raised voices replace respectful dialogue. Text messages become emotionally charged. Assumptions, accusations and interruptions take over.

At this point, it's not about solving anything, it's about being heard, being right or being vindicated. But at what cost? The reality is, when calmness disappears, logic quickly follows. You become emotionally flooded, and when that happens your child's needs are no longer front and centre.

Staying calm looks like:

- Taking time before responding to an emotional message
- Choosing to disengage from arguments that are unproductive or off-topic
- Speaking with clarity, not hostility.

Remember, instead of trying to match your co-parent's energy, focus on regulating yours.

2. C is for child-focused

> Keep your north star in sight.

Your child is the connection between you and your co-parent, and being child-focused must remain at the forefront of all your interactions. This means anchoring every discussion and decision around what your child needs, not what you want. It sounds obvious, but it's one of the easiest things to forget, especially when emotions become heightened and feelings from the past creep into present-day interactions.

When you're not child-focused, conversations tend to shift away from routines, well-being and developmental needs, and begin revolving around fairness, rights and ego. You've lost your focus on your child if:

- You say things that revolve around 'I', such as, 'I deserve' or 'I should', without considering how that might disrupt your child's stability.
- Your arguments are less about what benefits your child and more about punishing or outdoing your co-parent.
- Your child's emotional needs or preferences are barely being mentioned in conversations.

Your child's sense of safety and happiness must remain the priority. After all, they didn't choose to witness hostility, be a messenger or be placed in the middle. But staying child-focused is as simple as asking yourself: how will this decision impact my child's routine or emotional stability?

It's a powerful question that immediately shifts the spotlight away from ego, past hurts or the need to win an argument. It brings clarity in the chaos and anchors every decision in what truly matters: your child's well-being.

This mindset helps you move from reacting emotionally to responding intentionally, keeping your parenting aligned with your purpose – even when the relationship with your co-parent is strained.

3. C is for compromise

> Choose cooperation over control.

Compromise isn't weakness – it's maturity. It doesn't mean someone has lost – it means your child wins. It's not about being passive – it's about being emotionally intelligent and focused on long-term outcomes, not short-term wins.

It's the understanding that co-parenting is about making shared choices that serve your child. When both parents are willing to meet in the middle, it builds trust and shows your child that cooperation is possible, even after separation.

Some parents try to control every detail of the child's life, from schedules to who the child sees, what the child eats or even what brands the child is allowed to wear. This is often because of anxiety, distrust or unresolved hurt, but overly controlling behaviour tends to fuel conflict, not reduce it.

Healthy compromise shows your child that grown-ups can work together even when they don't always agree. It models teamwork, maturity and emotional resilience. Remember, you don't need to agree on everything – just enough to move forward together. Signs you're compromising well include:

- You're willing to adjust dates or times as and when emergencies come up.
- You acknowledge that your way isn't the only way.
- You try to meet in the middle on issues of parenting style whenever possible, without sacrificing your child's well-being.

Of course, not every situation is suited for compromise, especially when your child's safety is at risk, but many of the disagreements that cause friction could be resolved faster if both parents practised more flexibility and less defensiveness.

When you find yourself stuck in repeated cycles of conflict, ask yourself: which one of the 3 Cs have I forgotten about?

REFLECTION: PUTTING THE 3 Cs INTO PRACTICE

Think back to a recent or memorable conflict with your co-parent.

- Which of the 3 Cs did you move away from?
- What triggered that shift?
- What might you do differently now with the 3 Cs in mind?

The 3 Cs method isn't magic. It won't make your co-parent less difficult or undo years of tension, but it will help you show up as the consistent, grounded parent your child needs. The following exercise encourages you to enlist someone you trust to help you stick to the 3 Cs.

REFLECTION: STAYING ACCOUNTABLE

I want you to share what you've learned about the 3 Cs with a valued friend, family member or perhaps a therapist, because sometimes we need that extra accountability.

- Check in with them during tough co-parenting weeks.
- Talk through any recent moments when you strayed from the 3 Cs.
- Let them know your goal is to stick to the 3 Cs, even when it's hard.

Learning the hard way

When I look back on some of the most difficult disagreements or battles in my co-parenting journey, I can clearly see how the breakdown often came from one of us – usually me – losing sight of one of the 3 Cs.

There were times I didn't remain calm. My emotions got the better of me and I reacted from a place of frustration or hurt rather than clarity. There were moments I took my eyes off my child and made the situation about me, my feelings or my need to be heard or understood. And there were definitely times when I refused to compromise because I was convinced that my way was not just better, but it was, in fact, the only way.

These were the moments that prolonged the conflict, made communication harder and created tension that my child didn't deserve to feel, so if I'm sharing this with you now it's not because I've always got it right, but because I've learned the hard way what happens when you don't apply these principles.

#28

Economic abuse

When we talk about abuse in relationships, most people immediately think of verbal attacks or physical violence, but one of the most damaging and overlooked forms of abuse is economic abuse. Through my years of working as a co-parenting specialist, I've seen how many people fail to recognise financial manipulation as abuse. And I'll be honest, I was once one of them.

As mentioned, I remember once withholding money from my child's mum following an argument. It was my way of trying to control the situation and 'win', but what I failed to realise was that if my child's mum was struggling financially because of my actions, then not only was I committing this form of abuse, but I was also negatively impacting my child. Financial pressure impacts the home your child lives in, the food they eat, the activities they can take part in and the emotional stability they experience.

The money trap

When a relationship begins, some people will purposefully establish their financial power by covering all expenses, giving lavish gifts and paying for trips away, but this can be manipulation and control disguised as generosity and kindness. It may create a sense of security, but that can slowly become dependency.

And finances can certainly keep us trapped in relationships. For example, maybe you're unsure how you'd manage on just your income alone. Maybe you've built a lifestyle that relies on splitting costs. Or maybe you've become financially dependent, because the other parent has always provided the primary income.

This book isn't designed to explore every layer of economic abuse in detail, but it is vital that we talk about it within the context of co-parenting, because for many parents it becomes the main weapon used to maintain power, long after the intimate relationship has ended.

During a recent episode of the @Raisingboys2men podcast, child psychotherapist Daniella Kadene told me, 'A lot of people think that domestic abuse ends when the relationship does. But often, that's when it gets much worse. The break-up shatters the abuser's sense of control. They feel it slipping, their hold weakening, their power fading, and they can't take it, so they tighten their grip and do everything they can to hold on.'

This hit home for many of my audience members, but although Daniella's words may make some of you fearful of leaving a relationship, instead I need you to use the knowledge you'll gain from this chapter to better position yourself to fight against these types of individuals.

For many abusive ex-partners, separation doesn't signal the end of control; it removes the direct pathway they once had, so they search for another. And unfortunately, co-parenting, the family court system and the child maintenance framework (*see* pp. 140–141) give them plenty of opportunities to keep that control alive. Let's look at examples of how economic abuse can show up in co-parenting now.

Economic abuse in co-parenting

Economic abuse is any behaviour used to control a person's access to the financial resources they are entitled to, to limit their independence or to create instability that keeps them dependent. Keep that definition in mind as you look at the following examples:

Refusing to contribute financially

Some co-parents may refuse to make a monetary contribution to their child's upbringing as a way to exert control, punish the resident parent for ending the relationship or simply out of spite. They may agree to pay only if the resident parent meets certain demands.

This places an unfair financial burden on the resident parent and directly impacts the child's well-being.

Refusing to work or reducing hours to avoid paying
A co-parent may intentionally leave employment, reduce their hours or work 'off the books' to minimise their financial obligations. This behaviour can be a strategic attempt to avoid responsibility and undermine the other parent's ability to provide for the child.

Withholding earnings to avoid financial support
Some individuals deliberately hide income or pass money through others to make it appear they earn less than they do. This manipulative behaviour exploits loopholes in the system and directly harms the child, who depends on consistent financial support.

Using the legal system to drain the other parent financially
Some co-parents misuse the family court system as a weapon by repeatedly filing unnecessary applications, dragging out proceedings, withholding paperwork or repeatedly challenging agreed-upon terms. These tactics are designed to inflict financial strain through legal fees, missed work and emotional exhaustion. This is a recognised form of 'systems abuse', where legal structures are manipulated to maintain power.

It's crucial to recognise that financial support is a right of the child, not a favour to the resident parent. It should never be used as a tool for control or punishment, but setting up legally binding agreements and using systems that track and enforce payments can help protect resident parents and children from financial manipulation.

Economic abuse research

A major study of 540 Australian mothers revealed the scale of post-separation economic abuse in co-parenting. The findings – and I imagine they would be similar in most countries – paint a very disturbing picture with 79.8% of those surveyed reporting that their ex-partner used financial payments as a form of control. ▶

The same proportion (79.8%) also reported that their ex-partner had replaced physical abuse with abuse via child support as a way of controlling them after the relationship had ended.

When asked to choose from a list of 27 options regarding how their ex-partner controlled them through child support, the top three answers (selected by the 258 women who provided responses) were as follows:

- Reducing the amount of child support that they will pay, without your agreement (52.3%)
- Threatening to take you to the family court if you don't do what they want (45.0%)
- Deliberately not paying child support right before school fees are due, kids' birthdays and so on (35.3%).

Other answers included:

- Threatening to stop paying altogether if you don't do what they want
- Threatening you if you ask for child support payments
- Threatening to quit their job if you don't do what they want
- Threatening to put in a change of assessment if you don't do what they want.

How economic abuse affects children

Some parents truly believe that withholding money only harms their ex, failing to realise the direct impact that falls on the child. When a parent deliberately disrupts finances:

- The child may miss out on activities, clothing, school trips or basic needs.
- The primary parent becomes stressed, stretched or overwhelmed.
- The child learns that love, time and stability are conditional or weaponised.
- They internalise instability and insecurity.

Economic abuse is not just an attack on the parent, it is an attack on the child's well-being, security and emotional development. If you engage in these tactics you might think you're punishing the other parent, but in reality you're also hurting your child.

Providing occasional gifts or taking them on days out does not cover the everyday costs of raising a child. These expenses include:

- Extra utilities like gas and electricity
- Higher rent for a larger home to accommodate your child
- Refuelling the car to transport your child to school, activities and appointments.

If your child is anything like mine, or how I was as a child, then you also need to factor in the constant refilling of the fridge and cupboards, because our stomachs don't seem to have a limit!

Failing to contribute financially places unnecessary strain on the other parent, which inevitably affects the child. As I have said many times over, children pick up on emotional strain and, when a parent is struggling to make ends meet, the energy in the home changes.

I was aware of the financial strain in my home at a young age – not because my mum intentionally told me, but because I could feel it. I noticed when essentials were running low or when certain things I'd hoped for, like gifts at birthdays or Christmas, weren't possible. It wasn't something she ever wanted me to worry about, but the weight of it was unavoidable.

I remember my dad showing up occasionally, often with money in hand, as if it could replace his time. Once he even pulled out £40 in front of me, handed me £20 and said, 'That's for you and this is for me.' Looking back, it's moments like that that still linger – not just for their awkwardness, but because I felt a sense of responsibility that no child should carry.

Sometimes, I'd give that money to my mum, knowing it would help us at home. She never wanted to take it, but back then things were far harder than they are today, when there's more support available for single parents. My dad should have been more concerned about the stability of his son's home life and the well-being of the mother of his child than ensuring I had £20 to waste on football stickers or sweets.

As parents, our priority should always be making sure our child's home is stable, secure and as stress-free as possible – not whether they're dressed in the latest brands or if we look great as parents for buying them the newest FIFA game. What's the point of those things if the electricity is about to be cut off?

Open communication and cooperation between parents can alleviate many of the issues surrounding money, and if you're able to contribute, do so consistently and fairly. Your child deserves more than just the occasional treat; they deserve the peace of mind that comes with knowing both parents are fully committed to their well-being, financially and emotionally.

REFLECTION: YOUR EXPERIENCE OF ECONOMIC ABUSE

This exercise is designed to help you reflect honestly on your own experiences with child maintenance and financial behaviour in your co-parenting relationship. It's not about blame or finger pointing, it's simply about awareness, accountability and change moving forward.

Identify the behaviour

Read through the following statements and identify any that apply to your current or past situation – either actions you've experienced or behaviours you may have engaged in.

- I've used financial support as a way to get more access or control decisions about the child.
- I've refused to pay maintenance because I was unhappy with how my co-parent was spending the money.
- I've changed the amount I contribute depending on how I feel about my co-parent.
- I've threatened to stop paying if my demands aren't met.
- I've withheld financial support to 'teach the other parent a lesson.'

▶

- I've had child maintenance withheld, reduced or delayed due to arguments or personal conflict.
- I've experienced stress and instability because I never know what financial support is coming in.

Reflect on the behaviour

If you identified any statements that applied to you, how do you think this behaviour impacted your child's stability and well-being?

- What would you want from your co-parent if the roles were reversed?
- What can you do differently going forward, even if your co-parent isn't acting fairly?

Create a commitment statement

Make a vow to yourself and your child. It can be written down or simply spoken aloud and should outline how you will handle economic support moving forward. It should be centred around your child's needs, rather than your feelings about your co-parent.

If you're a non-resident parent, an example would be: 'My role to provide is a responsibility I have as a parent to my child and it will not be impacted by my emotions towards their other parent.'

If you are the primary parent, this could mean committing to this: 'Even if I feel hurt or frustrated by the lack of financial support, I will not let those feelings interfere with my child's relationship with their other parent.'

#29

A narcissist or just difficult?

The term 'narcissist' is often used, particularly on social media, when people are describing their co-parent, but it's important to differentiate between someone who is genuinely narcissistic in the clinical sense and someone who is simply emotionally reactive, petty or uncooperative.

According to the *Diagnostic and Statistical Manual of Mental Disorders (DSM-5)*, published by the American Psychiatric Association, narcissistic personality disorder (NPD) is defined as: 'A pervasive pattern of grandiosity (in fantasy or behaviour), need for admiration, and lack of empathy, beginning by early adulthood and present in a variety of contexts.' To receive a formal diagnosis, a person must meet at least five of the following nine criteria:

1. A grandiose sense of self-importance.
2. A preoccupation with fantasies of unlimited success, power, brilliance, beauty or ideal love.
3. A belief they are 'special' and can only be understood by, or associate with, other special or high-status people.
4. A need for excessive admiration.
5. A sense of entitlement.
6. A tendency to take advantage of others or be 'interpersonally exploitative'.
7. A lack of empathy.

8. An envy of others or belief that others envy them.
9. An arrogant attitude or haughty behaviour.

In addition, the Mayo Clinic notes that individuals with NPD often have troubled relationships and may be easily hurt by perceived criticism, despite appearing to have high self-esteem.

However, only around 1% of the population is estimated to have NPD, which means it's relatively rare. So, while it's not impossible to be co-parenting with someone who has the disorder, it's statistically more likely that you're dealing with someone who is simply emotionally difficult, reactive or immature, and that distinction matters.

Signs you may be dealing with a narcissistic co-parent are that they:

- May show consistent patterns of manipulation, gaslighting and using the child as a pawn
- Are unlikely to show genuine concern for the child unless it serves their image or control
- May weaponise the legal system, communication apps or court orders to maintain dominance
- Usually twist any attempts you make to compromise or reason with them or use them against you.

Dealing with this type of person will be emotionally exhausting and often isolating, and if this is your reality, know this: you're not crazy, weak or dramatic. You're dealing with someone who may never co-parent in a healthy way.

On the other hand, a difficult co-parent may:

- Be inconsistent, but occasionally cooperative
- React out of hurt, pride or mistrust, not a clinical disorder
- Struggle with boundaries, but still have a degree of empathy for the child
- Show signs of growth or willingness to improve with time, support or therapy.

Why you need to know the difference

Battling with a difficult co-parent can be one of the most emotionally taxing challenges you may face as a parent. It can leave you feeling drained, anxious, overwhelmed and, in extreme cases, it can even impact your ability to show up as the parent your child needs. That's exactly what makes this dynamic so dangerous, because it shifts your energy away from your child and towards your co-parent, and unnecessary conflict.

Often, the difficult co-parent's aim is to throw you off balance, creating emotional chaos and seeking reactions that can validate their own behaviour or agenda. This is why it's critical to approach these situations with clarity and intention.

Labelling someone a narcissist can make you feel less helpless or justify your combative responses, but because every behaviour is filtered through that characterisation communication often stops, because you believe change is impossible, even though there are tools that could improve the dynamic. Treating them as incapable of change can harden positions, escalate conflict and delay solutions that would benefit your child.

Understanding who you're really dealing with gives you back control. It doesn't excuse harmful behaviour, but it does allow you to respond strategically rather than emotionally. With a narcissistic co-parent, the aim becomes low contact, structured agreements and emotional detachment, not change, whereas with a difficult co-parent, communication tools and boundaries may eventually lead to better collaboration.

Don't fight fire with fire

I often hear from people asking if they should prevent the other parent from seeing their child or cut financial payments, because they're frustrated with the other parent's actions. This 'fire with fire' mentality causes far more damage than good and, most importantly, it's the child who ends up caught in the middle and hurt.

Imagine this:

- Your child, eagerly looking forward to spending time with their other parent, gets let down because you've chosen to block access. Their disappointment stems not from their other parent's inconsistency, but from a choice you've made out of frustration.
- Your child, who has a right to a relationship with both parents, now sees that right stripped away because unresolved issues between you and the other parent have taken precedence over their needs.
- Your child, living in a household now under financial pressure, because you've chosen to withhold support, feels the stress and anxiety of the other parent struggling to make ends meet. They sense the exhaustion, the tension, the weight, and it begins to impact their own emotional well-being.
- Your child is late for school because the stressed-out parent couldn't sleep properly, wasn't organised or couldn't function under the burden of financial insecurity. This causes your child to start the day feeling rushed, stressed and even embarrassed.

Whatever way you choose to look at it, fighting fire with fire only ends up burning the one person you both claim to care about most – your child. Rather than seeking revenge or reacting out of anger, focus on solutions that prioritise the child's well-being.

Your ability to remain calm, child-focused and willing to compromise (the 3 Cs – *see* pp. 145–150) will help ensure that your child grows up with the love, security and consistency they deserve, even in the face of co-parenting challenges.

Now, I wish simply saying 'don't fight fire with fire' was enough to solve the challenges of co-parenting, but the reality is far more complex. The truth is, there are many types of difficult co-parenting characters you might face or even become, and understanding their behaviours is the first step towards protecting your child and yourself from unnecessary harm.

While every situation is unique, there are patterns of behaviours that tend to emerge. By recognising these patterns you can equip yourself with the tools to navigate these challenges with clarity, composure and a focus on your child's well-being.

#30

The indirect communicator

You may have encountered some of the characters I spotlight in the next few chapters on your journey – or maybe you've been fortunate enough to avoid them altogether – but either way, for each type of difficult co-parent featured, I'll provide examples of their behaviours, how these actions may affect you and your child, and practical strategies to manage and mitigate their impact.

If your co-parent is what I call a messenger, they communicate indirectly, often using your child to relay messages instead of communicating directly with you. Whether it's about a schedule change or a significant concern, these messages often place unnecessary responsibility on the child, who is caught in the middle of adult conversations. This dynamic can lead to emotional strain, especially when the child feels like they are responsible for managing communication or keeping the peace.

For example, when my child was given a mobile phone at an early age, something I wasn't entirely comfortable with, I found myself using it to reach him when I couldn't get hold of his mum. I would ask him to pass on messages like, 'Can you ask your mum about X, Y or Z?' While these conversations were harmless, I quickly realised how easily my child was being placed in the middle of parental communication.

Even when there's no ill intent, this added responsibility can place unnecessary pressure on the child. Strained communication between parents often leads to telling the child to relay messages like, 'Tell your mum I'll pick you up on Saturday' or 'Let your dad know I need to talk to him about school.' While this might seem like a quick fix, it places your child in an uncomfortable and inappropriate position, often creating a situation where they are sent back and forth as a messenger.

Over time, this dynamic can also create unnecessary tension or misunderstanding between you and your co-parent. It's like a chain of miscommunication. By the time the message is delivered, it may be completely different from how it was originally intended, further complicating communication and increasing conflict.

As parents, we need to recognise that, especially when a clear routine is in place, there shouldn't be a need for lengthy or indirect communication. But when tensions rise, it's easy to fall into the habit of using the child as a messenger. This is something we must consciously avoid, to protect their emotional well-being. When used as messengers, they can feel torn between parents, unsure of how to deliver the message and anxious about disappointing either side.

How to navigate a messenger co-parent

There are a number of things you can do in this situation:

- Remain calm and avoid reacting negatively to your child, as they are not at fault.
- Gently remind your co-parent, in writing if necessary, that communication should happen directly between you as adults, not through the child.
- Consider using court-approved co-parenting apps that are available within your area. A simple Google search will help you identify suitable apps to help streamline communication in a neutral, documented space. These tools help maintain boundaries and prevent further misuse of your child as a messenger.

By addressing this behaviour constructively, you protect your child's emotional well-being and reinforce healthy boundaries, ensuring they can focus on being a child rather than managing adult responsibilities.

#31

Always the gatekeeper

The gatekeeper co-parent controls access to the child by setting unreasonable boundaries, withholding visitation, or using financial support as leverage. Their actions often stem from a need for control, prioritising their agenda over the child's right to a healthy and stable relationship with both parents.

For example, your co-parent decides to change or delay financial payments, sometimes withholding them altogether. You notice a pattern – this only seems to happen in months when you've disagreed on something or failed to meet their personal expectations. As discussed in chapter 28, while this behaviour may feel like a punishment directed at you, it's ultimately your child who suffers the consequences. The stress and anxiety placed on the primary parent, responsible for the child's well-being, trickles down to the child, impacting their stability and security.

Similarly, your co-parent might manipulate visitation schedules. They cancel your time with your child at the last minute or change agreed-upon plans without notice. These disruptions often coincide with disagreements or situations where they feel you haven't 'behaved' in a way they deem acceptable.

The gatekeeper's actions demonstrate a lack of concern for the emotional harm and instability this creates for the child. Their primary objective is to hurt or control you, often at the expense of your child's happiness and sense of security.

A word from Nieki Shaw, child protection lawyer

Nieki runs the social media platform @LegallyNik and is a child protection lawyer with over 14 years' experience. Here Nieki draws on that professional background to offer guidance on navigating high-conflict dynamics, alongside other legally complex issues that parents may face.

When considering how to respond to these behaviours, Nieki suggests the following actions:

Seek mediation or legal support

If gatekeeping around contact with your child becomes a persistent pattern and begins to affect their well-being it is important to consider mediation and, if necessary, legal intervention. The courts prioritise a child's best interests, and behaviour that restricts contact or undermines stability can be addressed through child arrangements or related orders.

Address financial gatekeeping formally if you have to

If gatekeeping of finances continues, serious consideration should be given to seeking a formal arrangement through the Child Maintenance Service (CMS). This is a government-run service that calculates child maintenance using a statutory formula, primarily based on the paying parent's income, the number of children and the level of overnight care. It can put a legally enforceable payment schedule in place, collect payments directly where required and take enforcement action if payments are missed. This removes the need for ongoing negotiation between parents and provides greater financial certainty for the child.

Document everything

Keep a detailed record of missed payments, altered visitation schedules and any unreasonable restrictions. This documentation may be helpful if legal intervention is necessary. ▶

Stay calm and consistent
Avoid reacting emotionally to their behaviour as this can escalate the situation. Maintain consistency in your interactions and remain focused on your child's needs. This will be a key priority if the matter were to ever require the court's attention and should therefore be practised as early as possible.

#32

Reliably inconsistent

We have already touched on the importance of consistency when raising a child (*see* pp. 72–74), but an inconsistent co-parent can be incredibly difficult to deal with. Their inconsistency may manifest as missed visits, failure to provide financial support or even emotional unpredictability when they are present. This behaviour often disrupts the child's routine, creates emotional confusion and places an additional burden on the resident parent.

While some of these actions may seem harmless in isolation, over time they build and create a sense of uncertainty for the child, who is often left disappointed or unsure of what to expect.

My father's inconsistency

When I was growing up, my father was extremely inconsistent. One day, when I was around nine, I remember him making a random appearance, showing up after years of avoidance, and taking me to a local KFC. I was thrilled, not just about the chicken and chips, but because I was finally spending time with my dad, a male figure I had longed for. He acknowledged that he hadn't been around and promised that things would change. He even mentioned plans to bring me and my sisters together; our relationship was non-existent due to his lack of accountability and unwillingness to merge families.

When I got home, I shared the conversation with my mum, who didn't seem too impressed, but was always happy if I was. I didn't realise it at the time, but she knew my father well. She knew his words didn't hold much weight and it most likely annoyed her that he was making promises she knew he wouldn't keep. Sure enough, after that visit, I didn't see him again for another four or five years. Looking back, I don't recall feeling a deep sense of loss. I mean, how do you miss someone who hasn't been a regular presence in your life?

Years later, around the age of 15, I remember walking home from a youth club and receiving a random phone call on my mobile from a number I didn't recognise. It was him. Hearing him say, 'Aaron, it's your dad' felt strange and to this day I don't feel comfortable calling him that. I call him by his name instead.

We arranged to meet again and for the next few years I experienced constant letdowns. I spent countless nights waiting by the window, watching every car that pulled up, hoping it was him, only to be disappointed time and time again. He said he would arrive at 6 p.m. so we could spend some quality time together, but that turned into a 10 p.m. visit where we sat in his car for five minutes and he handed me some form of financial compensation for his lack of time.

But through all of this, my mum never banished him from my life. She didn't prevent me from seeing him or block his number from my phone, but she never allowed him into our home, either. He could pick me up, take me out, but he was never allowed to get comfortable inside the home. This was a boundary I didn't fully understand as a child, but now, as an adult, I see her point. Why would you allow someone who has disrespected you and your child with their lack of effort and care to sit comfortably in your home?

My mum didn't interfere or make excuses for him; she let me see for myself who he was. She was always honest, supportive and there to catch me when his promises fell through. She showed me love when I felt none from him and gave me the space to make my own decision about whether I wanted to continue seeing him.

After years of disappointment, I withdrew. I no longer bought into his lies or sought his attention. I had other positive male influences around me, like my barber, Vinton, who took me under his wing from the age of 13. His barber shop became a place where I learned about manhood, watching how men laughed, communicated and supported each other. That space gave me a blueprint of how men should behave – something I didn't get from my father, but from the community of good men that attended that shop.

Stopping contact

A question I hear often is: should I stop contact if the other parent continues to be inconsistent? This can be a challenging dilemma, especially when your child is repeatedly let down by the other parent, but, legally, cutting off contact should only be done in situations where there is a genuine risk to the child's safety or well-being.

In most cases, the answer is an extremely personal one, but predominantly lies in setting boundaries that protect your child from emotional harm while still maintaining their relationship with the other parent. The key is to create structure and predictability where there is little. Here are some practical boundaries you can implement:

Don't inform the child until the day of the visit

Children often feel the most hurt when they're left waiting for a parent who never shows up. To protect them from this disappointment, one boundary could be to only tell the child about the visit on the day it's supposed to happen.

This way, if the inconsistent parent cancels or doesn't show up, the child isn't left waiting, because they were never aware that anything had been scheduled in the first place. While you can't control how the other parent behaves, you do have control over what information your child is given and when. That, in itself, is a powerful way of protecting them.

Set a rule that the inconsistent parent must confirm the visit a few hours before the scheduled time. Only when the confirmation is received should the child be told about the visit. If the other parent still cancels or doesn't show up – even after confirming – it can be heartbreaking for both you and your child. However, by limiting the build-up, you reduce the emotional impact of the let-down. Although you're not preventing disappointment altogether, you're softening the blow.

Some parents may choose to make visits a complete surprise, only telling their child when the other parent is moments away. Others find a different approach works better for their family. There's no single right answer here, because every child and every situation is different.

What matters most is that each time your child's expectations are shattered, you step in to comfort them and be the consistent, safe and loving parent that the other is failing to be. Part of this is recognising that you cannot always shield your child from the disappointment of an inconsistent parent, but you can soften those moments for them – and that is where your parenting truly shows.

Set a clear schedule

Inconsistent parents may feel entitled to show up whenever they want, which can create chaos for both the child and the other parent. By enforcing a strict schedule you create a framework that both the child and the inconsistent parent must follow. This helps bring predictability to an otherwise unpredictable situation.

To implement this, agree on specific visitation days and times. If the inconsistent parent misses or cancels the visit, the next opportunity is at the next scheduled time. This rule helps the child maintain a sense of routine and prevents last-minute disruptions.

Empower your child

My mother's approach of allowing me to make my own decisions about my father while protecting me emotionally taught me the true value of boundaries. She didn't shield me from the reality of his inconsistency or make excuses for him. Instead, she empowered me to see the truth for myself, while providing a safe and loving environment to come back to when I needed support.

This balance was crucial. It allowed me to experience the reality of my father's actions, but without the bitterness or resentment that might have come if she had actively blocked me from seeing him. She never spoke ill of him, nor did she impose her opinions on me. Her approach gave me the room to make my own judgements about his role in my life, which, in turn, helped me build resilience and emotional maturity. At the same time, she was always there to cushion the fall when his promises broke down. She didn't try to control the situation or force decisions upon me, but she never let his behaviour affect how she showed up for me as a parent.

It can be incredibly difficult to watch your child face disappointment, especially when you know it's avoidable, but allowing them to experience these emotions within a protective framework helps them develop a deeper understanding of relationships, reliability and trust. Think of it this way: allowing your child to see the other parent for who they are, with boundaries in place, gives them the chance to understand the situation with clarity rather than confusion. By maintaining a balanced approach, you're helping your child develop emotional strength and the ability to manage disappointment – skills that will serve them throughout their lives.

Your consistent presence in your child's life will make up for the inconsistencies of the other parent. You alone are enough. What's more, children are incredibly resilient and, even if they experience disappointment, your steady love and support will be the foundation that guides them through. That stability is a priceless gift, one that they will carry with them into adulthood.

How to navigate an inconsistent co-parent

Here are some top tips to help you handle this situation:

- Establish clear expectations with the co-parent, even if they are unreliable. Keep communication professional and child-focused, using written forms like email or co-parenting apps to document interactions.
- Be honest (but age-appropriate) with your child. Acknowledge their feelings when their parent disappoints them and offer child-centric reassurance without making excuses.

- Create a stable routine. Provide as much predictability as possible in your own household to offset the instability caused by the inconsistent co-parent.
- Avoid making promises on your co-parent's behalf. Don't set your child up for disappointment by confirming plans unless you are sure they will follow through.
- Write everything down. Keep a record of missed visits, changes in plans and financial support issues. This documentation can be helpful if legal action becomes necessary.
- Seek support when needed. If the inconsistency becomes harmful to your child's emotional well-being, consider mediation or legal advice to formalise visitation and financial agreements.

By staying calm, maintaining a stable environment and modelling resilience for your child, you can offset the damage caused by an inconsistent co-parent. Remember, your steady presence will provide the security your child needs.

#33

The pixel-perfect co-parent

Consistency isn't glamorous. It doesn't get likes on social media. But what children remember when they're older is the person who shows up at parents' evening, who knows the names of their teachers, who packs the spare socks and remembers the appointment times. That's what shapes their sense of safety.

I've had people tell me many stories about their co-parents, including those whose sole focus seemed to be how they appeared on social media. One, for instance, described how their co-parent would show up with smiles and gifts, and film the excitement, but vanish for weeks at a time. Then, when a birthday or holiday rolled around, they would suddenly reappear, phone in hand, ready to film a 'Daddy and me' moment for Instagram. The child would light up when he saw his dad, but he was young and didn't understand, and it was crystal clear this wasn't really about the child, it was about image.

The father would tag his co-parent in stories, as though the two were a functional co-parenting unit, but she was the one left explaining why Daddy didn't call back and comforting her son when he cried after another missed weekend visit. Ultimately, though, she made a decision to stop engaging with the performance. She stopped sharing the clips. She didn't co-sign the narrative. She didn't badmouth him either, but focused on teaching her son, through example, that love shows up even when no one's watching.

This scenario is a clear example of a parent who prioritised image and external validation over their child's emotional needs. Dealing with a co-parent like this is undoubtedly challenging, but, particularly with the prevalence of social media, it's important to keep in mind the following points.

How to navigate a social media parent

There are several things you can do if your co-parent falls into this category:

- Avoid reacting emotionally to posts, videos or comments.
- Prioritise your child's emotional stability over social media narratives.
- Limit opportunities for the other parent to use the child for content.
- Unfollow or block them on social media, to reduce the chance of them using your posts and to protect yourself from being negatively affected by false narratives.
- If they are inappropriate, report any images to the relevant social media site.

For the parent performing for social media there are lessons to be learned, too:

- Understand that focusing on image rather than presence can confuse the child about what love really is.
- Social media performances should never replace genuine parenting.
- Remember that your child is learning from real-life interactions with you, not the 'Instagram-perfect' moments you display.
- A child learns about love, reliability and trust through consistent, everyday acts, not photo opportunities or staged moments.

While social media can amplify unhealthy co-parenting behaviours, setting boundaries, staying calm and keeping a child-centred focus can mitigate the damage. Both parents share the same responsibility: to engage consistently, genuinely, and in a way that protects the child from confusion and emotional harm.

Finally, if you find it necessary, there are legal options available should you feel uncomfortable with your child's images being shared online. You are encouraged to seek independent legal advice to assess the merits of your individual circumstances.

#34

Children need two parents

Your child is a combination of both of you, not just in appearance, but in temperament, habits and emotional make-up. They wouldn't exist without the contribution of both parents, which is why you are both just as important, regardless of how you feel towards each other.

Think of it like baking a cake. What's more important – the flour or the eggs? Each ingredient brings something unique to the mix. Remove one and the result is completely different. The same goes for parenting. If we spend our time arguing over whose contribution matters more, or trying to replicate only our childhood experiences, we miss the opportunity to create something greater together – a balanced upbringing that combines the best of both of us.

Your child deserves the richness that comes from both ingredients. Not one overpowering the other, but both working together to help raise them into a healthy adult. Your child benefits most when both parents bring their unique contributions, not just shaped by gender but by experience, knowledge, wisdom and love.

Your way isn't the only way

We're all different and it's easy to fall into the trap of believing our way is the right way. I struggled with this at the start of my co-parenting journey. Growing up with an amazing single mum, I was used to things being done a certain way, with specific rules, routines and a lifestyle that I thought was 'normal', but the truth is, normal is subjective.

That version of normal isn't better, it's just familiar. Real growth in co-parenting comes when you recognise the strengths and weaknesses in your own upbringing and remain open to the perspective of your co-parent. Because the goal isn't to recreate your childhood or their childhood, it's to build something new that works for your child.

When both parents are willing to collaborate, put their egos aside, and combine their experiences to prioritise their child's needs over personal preferences, that's where the magic happens. The right way isn't always your way – it's the way that best serves your child, not the child you once were.

Every parent brings something different to the table. These differences are often deeply rooted in our own childhood experiences, shaped by the homes we grew up in, the roles we were asked to play and the relationships that either nurtured or neglected us.

These aren't just personality traits or habits; they're survival responses and emotional defaults. They're learned behaviours we carry into adulthood and parenting, often without even realising. When we begin to recognise and respect these differences, rather than compete with or criticise them, we give our child the gift of a balanced upbringing – one shaped not by ego, but by awareness.

Two upbringings, one approach

Let me give you a real example. As I've mentioned throughout, I was raised by a single mother. My father's presence was sporadic at best and I didn't have a relationship with my three half-siblings. I stepped into the 'man of the house' role far earlier than any child should have to, but as an only child I also got away with a lot, most likely because my mum was overcompensating for the absence of my dad. I was deeply loved, but that love came with a kind of protection that left me underprepared – not emotionally, but practically.

Now contrast that with my youngest child's mother. She was raised in a two-parent household. Both her mum and dad were present and active. She's the eldest of four children and shares a strong, ongoing bond with her siblings. From early on, she cooked meals, did chores and stepped in as a caregiver for her younger siblings.

She had structure where I had uncertainty. She had teamwork where I had independence. She had the consistent presence of a father where I had the consistent absence of mine. Her bond with her siblings remains strong, built on shared experience and family unity. My siblings and I were raised in different homes with no real connection.

These aren't minor differences. They're polar opposites. Now imagine if we were both fighting to prove which upbringing was better – each of us trying to replicate the exact same feeling, love and routine we were given as a child. That would be a nightmare – not just for us, but most of all for our child. Instead, we have worked together to create a new version of normal for our child – one that draws from the strengths we both bring, as individuals and as products of our own lived experiences.

The problem I see too often in co-parenting is this: parents who are either trying to recreate their childhood or are refusing to acknowledge that their co-parent was raised entirely differently.

Even if you were both raised in two-parent homes, had the same number of siblings, lived on the same street and even shared a birthday, I promise you that your upbringings were still different. Your stories, emotions, traumas and experiences were your own, and all of that shapes the adults and the parents you've become.

To co-parent effectively you have to let go of the belief that your way is the only way – that your childhood was better or more valid than your co-parent's – because real growth in co-parenting begins the moment you stop competing with the past and start building something better, together.

Complement each other

The goal for you and your co-parent isn't to parent identically, it's to parent intentionally. That means approaching parenting with self-awareness, respect for each other's pasts and a shared commitment to raising a well-rounded child.

You may not always agree, and your approaches might look different, but that doesn't mean one is better than the other. What matters is the intention behind your choices and the impact they have on your child.

I've learned to focus less on trying to be the 'fun' parent and more on finding ways to create balance. Take Easter, for example. Years ago, I would've rushed out to buy the biggest egg I could find, as if there was a prize for who could fill our child's stomach with the most chocolate, even though I wouldn't eat that much sugar myself.

I realise now that my child's mum has a much bigger family than I do and, naturally, he'll receive plenty of treats from them. So instead of competing, I've shifted my focus. I now look for meaningful, alternative ways to make memories with him that don't involve excess or comparison.

Another way I parent with intention is by checking in on how his week has been before our time together. Has he been staying up late? Had more screen time than usual? Eaten lots of sweets? If so, I gently bring the balance back. Maybe we'll cut out the sweets for the weekend, read a bit more or aim for earlier bedtimes to help him reset and feel ready for the week ahead.

Some parents become so focused on outdoing each other that the child ends up overstimulated and unbalanced, but here's the beauty in all of this – it only takes one of you to create balance. Even if the other parent has a different approach, you can still bring calm, routine and awareness to your child's world. That's a quiet kind of power. You just have to be willing to pay attention to what's going on when your child is away from you – not to judge, but to understand and respond with care.

Routine issues

A common flashpoint that often arises in co-parenting is the difference in routine between households. I often hear from parents who share how, when their child is with the non-resident parent, bedtime gets pushed later, screen time increases and rules seem to slip away. Sometimes, this may be the other parent's way of trying to feel like the 'fun one' or to bond without the boundaries that come with day-to-day structure.

If you're the parent who carries the weight of the weekday routine – the early mornings, the school prep, the emotional regulation and everything in between – I want you to know I see you. I understand how exhausting it can feel to spend the first part of the week undoing tiredness or calming overstimulation, while still trying to keep things positive and grounded for your child.

It's okay to feel frustrated – you're human – but you're not alone in this. Yes, it would be ideal if routines were aligned across both homes. That consistency would make things easier, no doubt. But even in the differences there's something valuable being offered to your child. Over time, they begin to experience and understand contrast. They start to notice how it feels to be well-rested versus overtired. They start to realise the impact of structure, even if they don't yet have the words for it.

What you're doing matters. The routine, the boundaries, the calm space you're building – even when they go unnoticed – are shaping the foundation your child returns to. It may not always feel appreciated now, but it will be felt later. So keep showing up with love and intention. Keep offering the rhythm they can rely on. Your efforts are not in competition with the other home – they are a gift your child will come to value in ways you may not yet see.

I recently asked my audience on social media to share examples where they and their co-parent had opposing approaches to parenting. One response really stood out. It came from a mother who is vegan, while her child's other parent eats mainly meat, eggs and dairy. These are two completely different lifestyles, not just in food preference, but in values and beliefs, too.

I asked whether these differences existed during the relationship, and she explained that while they were together she typically handled the cooking and her partner would simply eat what she prepared. She also felt reassured by the fact that his wider family were either vegetarian or vegan, and together they agreed their child would be raised as a vegetarian, at least until they were old enough to make their own decisions.

But since the separation this agreement hasn't been upheld. The father now feeds their child according to his own dietary choices during his parenting time. Understandably, this has caused frustration for the mother and it's a reminder that you cannot control what happens in the other parent's home. What you can do, however, is offer balance. You can create consistency and clarity in your own home, model your values and trust that over time your child will develop the awareness to make informed choices for themselves.

This isn't about winning or enforcing your way. It's about raising a child who understands that different perspectives exist and giving them the tools, exposure and space to find their own.

REFLECTION: UNDERSTANDING WHAT YOU BOTH BRING

The purpose of this exercise is to see the value in what you both bring to the table and how your child can benefit from this.

- Take some time to reflect on your own upbringing. Ask yourself:
  - What values and practices from my childhood do I cherish and want to pass on?
  - What behaviours or patterns do I want to avoid repeating?
- Create a 'keep and change' list, because writing it down can help you achieve clarity.
- Then try to observe (or even ask) what your co-parent brings from their own childhood.
  - What are they doing well that you hadn't considered before?

* What might be a fear or trigger that's affecting their parenting?
* How do your differences complement each other?

If your relationship is healthy enough for it, you could even share these reflections with one another. Highlight the overlaps and differences, and find the sweet spot that works best for your child.

#35

Enter the red zone

Most of us have heard of the term 'red flag'. It's a warning sign telling us to walk away from a situation or person, but my problem with red flags is that they are waved *after* an incident has occurred. For example, in football a red card is shown as the result of a serious foul being committed, by which point a player may be badly injured.

That's why, in this section, I am shifting the focus away from reacting to problems to preventing them in the first place. Instead of waiting for red flags to appear, I want to help you identify your co-parenting red zones. These are those personal triggers or boundaries that, if crossed, can escalate tension, cause conflict or lead to emotional harm in your co-parenting relationship. Once you become aware of your red zones, you can take proactive steps to avoid them or minimise their impact.

What is a red zone?

A red zone isn't a specific incident, it's a space, setting or scenario where you consistently feel tension, discomfort or are more likely to experience conflict with your co-parent. These areas will be different for everyone, including your co-parent. What may be a red zone for you could be an area where your co-parent doesn't feel triggered at all. This difference in perspective can sometimes be the very reason conflict arises.

Red zones are environments where your communication tends to break down or where emotions run high. For example, a red zone might be speaking to your co-parent on the phone, especially if conversations often turn heated or unproductive. It could be in-person handovers, where body language or tone create friction, or attending school events together, where unresolved feelings may surface.

These spaces act as emotional minefields, not because of what always happens, but because of what tends to happen. Identifying your red zones gives you the opportunity to prepare for, adapt to or even avoid them altogether, helping you stay grounded and protecting the co-parenting relationship from unnecessary harm.

Common red zones

Before we dive into specific examples, it's important that you take a moment to reflect on your own experiences. Red zones are personal and yours will be shaped by your unique relationship dynamics and history. Think back to moments of tension or conflict with your co-parent. Were there certain topics that consistently led to frustration or emotional reactions?

While I can't define your exact red zones for you, I can highlight some of the most common ones shared with me by others navigating the co-parenting journey, particularly those who follow and engage with my work on social media. I can also provide some suggestions for how to manage these situations.

The following scenarios aren't guaranteed to be red zones for you, but they are spaces that, based on experience, can become red zones if the right boundaries aren't in place. By exploring them, you may start to identify areas in your own situation where proactive steps could make a big difference.

Phone discussions

These can be red zones because:

- Phone calls allow for immediate, unfiltered emotional reactions, which can quickly escalate conflicts.
- You may often feel overpowered during conversations and not given the space to actually speak – you are simply spoken to.

- There's no written record of what was said, which can lead to misunderstandings or disputes later on.
- Tone and emotion are easily misinterpreted, especially when there's already tension between you.

Example: You call your co-parent to confirm pick-up arrangements for the weekend. However, before even receiving an answer you are hit with, 'Where did you go last time I had the kids?' You respond vaguely, but they press further, asking who you were with. You remind them that your personal life has nothing to do with your parenting, especially when it doesn't involve your child. Instead of dropping it, they accuse you of being secretive and disrespectful. You find yourself defending choices that have nothing to do with your role as a parent. The conversation quickly spirals into a heated debate, leaving you angry, drained and without the answer you originally called for.

How to manage it: Recognising that phone calls between you and your co-parent are a red zone allows you to avoid them and instead opt for other forms of communication, such as email, texting or even using a co-parenting app. Choosing not to engage in this way doesn't impact anyone's ability to parent or see their child, but it does help protect your peace. You can also prepare for phone conversations that can't be avoided. Having an exit strategy ensures you can step away from these situations with your mental well-being intact.

- Set boundaries early: 'I'm happy to discuss our child, but I won't be answering personal questions that don't involve them.'
- If the tone shifts or becomes confrontational, calmly say, 'Let's end this conversation and I'll follow up in writing.' Then end the call before it escalates further.

In-person handovers

These can be red zones because:

- Seeing your co-parent can bring up unresolved emotions.
- Tension can be high during handovers, especially if there's unresolved conflict.

- These moments can be emotionally charged and even a small comment can escalate into a bigger issue.
- The presence of your child can add pressure. You're trying to model good behaviour while internally managing frustration or hurt.
- The child may feel uncomfortable or caught between their parents.

Example: You arrive for the handover and greet your child warmly, but your co-parent barely acknowledges you. As you help your child into the car, they make a passive-aggressive comment like, 'You're actually on time for once.' You try to brush it off, but they follow it up with, 'Please make sure they have something healthy for dinner – none of that rubbish you normally give them.' Suddenly, what should have been a quick transition turns into a tense, awkward moment with your child stuck in the middle. You leave feeling flustered, angry and deflated for the rest of the day.

How to manage it: When things were at their most tense between me and my eldest son's mother, she chose to use her mum's house as my collection or drop-off point when spending time with my son, I now understand how necessary this was for her mental well-being. This kept her clear of the red zone and it had no impact on my ability to see my son. In fact, looking back, it actually made things easier. This won't be an option for everyone, maybe due to distance or the availability of your own parents, but perhaps you have friends or other family members who could help. And if that's not possible and you find yourself in the red zone, you're now better equipped to manage it.

- Keep handovers short, polite and focused solely on the child.
- Have your child ready beforehand to minimise interaction time.
- If comments are made, try not to engage emotionally in the moment, especially if your child is within earshot – remember you are there to collect or receive your child.
- If needed, pre-agree handover arrangements in writing, so expectations are clear before you even meet.

- If tensions remain high, consider neutral handover locations, like school drop-offs or kids' clubs, to create a more structured, less emotionally charged exchange.

Financial discussions

These can be red zones because:

- Money can trigger strong emotions, especially if one parent feels unsupported or the other feels unfairly burdened.
- Conversations around finances often carry underlying resentment, especially when there's a lack of transparency or trust.
- If financial agreements are unclear, it can create confusion and resentment.
- These discussions can blur boundaries – what's about the child versus what's about control or proving a point.

Example: You bring up the cost of an upcoming school trip in a message, asking if your co-parent can contribute half. Their response? 'I already pay child maintenance. Take it out of that.' You try to explain that this is an extra cost outside regular maintenance, but their tone quickly shifts. Suddenly, you're being accused of mismanaging money. Before you know it, the conversation has spiralled into an argument about who pays for what, how often and who's more involved. The original subject of the message – the school trip – gets completely lost.

How to manage it: The truth is, some parents will only ever pay child maintenance and nothing more (*see* chapter 28), but when heading into conversations like this, acceptance can be one of your most powerful tools. You're not there to convince or argue. You're simply asking a question and looking for a 'yes' or 'no'. Fortunately, there are a few ways to approach these discussions more effectively.

- Keep financial discussions child-focused and factual. Stick to specific amounts, dates and reasons.
- Avoid discussing money during emotionally heightened moments such as handovers or phone calls. Use written communication where possible.

- Set clear agreements in writing where you can, even if it's informal. Clarity avoids conflict.
- Consider using a shared parenting app with a built-in expense tracker to reduce misunderstandings.

REFLECTION: MAPPING YOUR RED ZONES

Before you can change how you respond to conflict, you first need to understand where that conflict is most likely to arise. This task is designed to help you identify your red zones and prepare strategies to manage or avoid them. Avoid rushing when reviewing these questions. Even if you feel the answers are obvious, spend some time sitting with them. The insights you uncover can be powerful tools in protecting your peace and creating a healthier co-parenting dynamic.

Identify your red zones

- Think back over the past few months or even years. What situations consistently led to tension or conflict between you and your co-parent?
  - Are there certain places, for example handovers at the house or school events?
  - Certain times, for example late at night, early mornings or during work hours?
  - Certain methods of communication, for example phone calls or voice notes?
  - Are there specific topics that almost always result in arguments?
- Write down at least two red zones you've identified from your own experience.

Reflect on the impact

- For each red zone you listed above, ask yourself:
  - How do I usually feel after being in that situation?

▶

* How does it affect my mood, parenting or ability to stay calm?
* How does it impact my child, even indirectly?

Create your red zone plan

- Now that you're aware of your red zones, how can you better manage them moving forward? For each red zone, answer:
  * Can this be avoided or changed, for example by using email instead of phone calls?
  * What boundary can I set – for example, 'I won't discuss finances during handovers'?
  * What's your exit strategy – for example, 'If it escalates, I'll politely end the call and follow up in writing.'

Remember, you can't control what your co-parent says or does, but you can control your awareness, your boundaries and your response.

#36

Alienation effect

Parental alienation is the deliberate manipulation or coercion of a child by one parent towards the other. There is currently no legal definition for this, so it can be a complex case to bring to court, but parental alienation is real and its effects on a child can be profound.

If you choose to restrict access to or cut off the other parent, make sure it's for reasons that truly serve your child's well-being and that it's not out of your own personal frustration. It should never be because someone missed a child maintenance payment, moved on to a new relationship or chose to have another child. Reacting emotionally to situations like these may feel justified in the moment, but it can have lasting consequences for your child.

Of course, we are all prone to making reactive decisions, responding to a situation in the heat of the moment and regretting it later. But now, with a child caught in the middle, every choice you make must be with their best interests at heart. Gone are the days when this was just about you and your ex. Co-parenting is about putting your child's needs first, even when it's hard and even when it feels unfair.

It's important to understand that parental alienation isn't just limited to conflicts between parents. It can involve other family members, such as grandparents, siblings, aunts and uncles, who may also influence the child's perception of the alienated parent, sometimes without even realising it. This behaviour doesn't just hurt the relationship between the child and the alienated parent, it fractures the entire family dynamic. Parents who engage in alienating behaviours may display signs such as:

- Constantly belittling or undermining the other parent
- Limiting or blocking communication between the child and the other parent

- Forbidding the child from discussing the other parent or making them feel guilty for doing so
- Portraying the other parent as unloving or unimportant
- Subtly or directly influencing the child to reject the other parent.

Parental alienation isn't something I've personally experienced, but I've certainly had moments of frustration where I threw around the phrase, 'You're stopping me from seeing my child.' Looking back, I realise that this wasn't true. My child's mum wasn't actively trying to keep me away. She just wasn't willing to accommodate unreasonable demands, such as me showing up at her home unannounced.

It's crucial to recognise the difference between a conflict over boundaries (*see* chapter 17) and true parental alienation. True alienation happens when one parent actively obstructs the child's relationship with the other parent, often through manipulation, rejection or preventing contact altogether. In contrast, situations like being told, 'Not today, I have plans' or having to navigate logistical conflicts don't fall under the umbrella of parental alienation. These are temporary issues that can be worked through.

How alienation works

Parental alienation is more common than we often realise. In the UK, 200 children lose contact with a parent each day due to parental alienation, with one in three children never seeing their alienated parent again after divorce or separation. In the US, studies show that at least 3.9 million children are moderately to severely alienated from a parent. However, although we often associate parental alienation with fathers, it's not a gender issue. Alienation happens to both mothers and fathers, and to boys and girls.

The impact on the child

When a child is alienated from one parent, the effects can be severe and long-lasting. The child may experience:

- Difficulty controlling their emotions, leading to impulsivity or outbursts
- Disturbed sleep cycles
- Poor academic performance
- Mimicking the alienating parent's behaviour into adulthood
- Anxiety, distress and a lack of emotional intelligence
- Psychological trauma from the behaviours of one or both parents.

The impact isn't just emotional – it also affects the child's ability to develop healthy relationships, as they may internalise the belief that rejecting a parent is acceptable.

Italian researchers found that individuals who were exposed to parental alienating behaviours as children had a higher likelihood of developing low self-esteem, perceiving only negative aspects of situations or having poorer coping skills in stressful environments. They also found an association between depression in adults and reported exposure to alienating parental behaviours in childhood.

The impact on the alienated parent

Parents who experience alienation may suffer from severe emotional distress, including anxiety and feelings of helplessness. These individuals can experience feelings of worthlessness and emotional pain, contributing to higher rates of depression. The emotional distress caused by parental alienation can increase the risk of suicidal ideation and self-harm. In one study, 54% of targeted parents had ideations of suicide, and in another, 24% of study participants had actually attempted it.

Being alienated from your child can also lead to a loss of parental identity, as the alienated parent may feel like they no longer have a role in their child's life. This can be devastating, particularly for parents who strongly identify with their role as caregivers.

In short, parental alienation is not a topic to take lightly. The emotional toll it exacts on both the child and the alienated parent is profound and often long-lasting.

What if I am accused of parental alienation?

If you find yourself being accused of parental alienation it's essential to approach the situation with self-awareness, patience and a willingness to listen. Here's what you can do:

Open the conversation

Start by calmly asking the other parent to clarify the specific behaviours or actions they've observed that lead them to believe you're alienating them. This isn't about placing blame, it's about understanding their concerns and seeing where things might have gone wrong.

Reflect on their concerns and try not to become defensive. Acknowledging their perspective can help to diffuse tension and lead to more productive discussions. Take time to assess your own behaviour and your interactions with your child and the other parent. Ask yourself questions like:

- Have I made negative remarks about the other parent in front of my child?
- Have I unintentionally allowed my personal frustrations to influence how I speak about or interact with the other parent?
- How can I present a more positive image of the other parent for the sake of my child's well-being?

Reflecting on your actions helps you see if any unconscious behaviours are contributing to the situation.

Speak more positively about the other parent

If you recognise that you've expressed negative opinions about the other parent, it's important to correct that behaviour.

Going forward, focus on speaking positively (or neutrally) about the other parent, especially when your child is present.

Seek mediation or therapy

If the situation remains difficult, you might consider suggesting family therapy or mediation. A neutral third party can help facilitate better communication and guide you both towards more collaborative co-parenting strategies.

What if I am being alienated?

If you are the one being alienated, it's important to act strategically and protect your relationship with your child, while also addressing the behaviour. Here's how you can move forward:

Document everything

Begin by keeping detailed records of any instances that might suggest alienation. This includes any negative comments made by the other parent about you in front of your child, instances where your visitation or communication is restricted without a valid reason or any manipulative behaviours that may be causing emotional harm to your child.

Keep a journal or use a co-parenting app that allows you to log communications, issues related to visitation or concerns you might have. Documentation will be useful if you need to take legal action.

Remain focused on your child's emotional well-being

It's crucial to maintain a supportive and emotionally available relationship with your child during this time. Make sure they feel heard and loved by you, despite the situation. Avoid speaking negatively about the other parent in front of them, as this could worsen the alienation.

Obtain legal advice

If the alienation persists or becomes severe, it may be necessary to seek legal intervention. Consult a family lawyer to discuss your options, which may include filing a motion to modify any parenting plan or requesting supervised visitation if the alienation is putting your child at risk emotionally or psychologically.

Legal intervention should be considered a last resort and it's important to approach this step with a clear understanding of how it will impact the child.

Be consistent and patient

Consistency and patience in your efforts to maintain a healthy, supportive relationship with your child are key. It may take time to repair any damage, but it is possible to rebuild the connection.

Regularly check in with your child to ensure they feel supported and continue demonstrating through actions that you are present and reliable, even if the situation feels out of your control.

It's essential to understand the difference between normal co-parenting conflict and intentional alienation. Normal co-parenting conflict is when both parents struggle to get along at times but still support the child having a relationship with both, whereas intentional alienation is when one parent *deliberately* tries to damage or prevent the child's relationship with the other parent.

When any type of conflict arises, it's important to pause and consider the long-term consequences of your actions on your child's emotional and psychological well-being. Our role as parents is to support our child's relationship with both parents, not to stand in the way of that connection, even when it's difficult.

#37

Therapy could be for you

Therapy is a taboo topic for many. However, engaging in therapy or reflective practices can significantly impact the quality of your co-parenting and the way your child is raised. As parents, when we take the time to process our past experiences and address unresolved issues, we are better equipped to parent with intention rather than reaction.

Research shows that parents who understand their own childhood experiences and emotional patterns are better able to recognise how these may influence their parenting. Self-reflection and therapeutic support can help you respond with greater awareness, rather than unconsciously repeating negative cycles from your own upbringing.

Therapy was something my mum consistently encouraged me to pursue from a very young age. In hindsight that makes total sense, but in my mind I was always fine. I thought, you can't change the past, so why revisit something you can't change? Surely it was just about getting on with life? But the truth is the past shapes us in ways we can't always see, and healing is about understanding and working through that rather than ignoring it.

Although I was unaware of the above benefits before I began my therapy journey, I can honestly say therapy has profoundly changed my understanding of how my past has shaped not only the person I am today, but also the way I view my children and how they see me.

Be the parent your child needs

As a child, I loved football and was a massive Chelsea FC fan, but with my dad not being around I always felt like I missed out on that classic father-and-son-bonding-over-sport experience. I envied my cousin going off to matches and football training with his dad, and seeing the impact of his dad's presence alongside the absence of mine, I made a silent promise to myself that when I had kids they would be into football.

From the moment my boys were born, I had Chelsea kits printed with their names on the back. I signed them up for training sessions and did my best to nudge – and at times push – them into the sport. But it wasn't until I started therapy that I realised something important: I was being the father I wanted to be, not necessarily the father they needed.

Truth is, they just weren't that into football – or really that good – but what they did love was art, Marvel and gaming. All the things I probably would've overlooked had I continued focusing on what I missed out on. So now, instead of forcing my football dreams on to them, I focus on who they actually are as individuals. And because of that our quality time looks completely different and, to be honest, is so much better.

With Omari, that might mean heading to the gym at 6 a.m. to get a workout in or going out to a hip hop concert together. I love the fact that we enjoy some of the same artists; it gives us even more moments we can genuinely share.

As for Tyler, we take trips to the comic store, catch the latest movie releases and when the weather's right we'll head to a theme park. Now, I'll be real, I am not a theme park fan. The queues, the rides, the chaos ... none of it is for me. But Tyler? He absolutely thrives there. His face lights up in a way that reminds me exactly why I'm putting up with it.

Therapy helped me understand that I was projecting my childhood wounds on to my children, trying to heal through them rather than for them. And in doing that, I was missing out on the opportunity to connect with their world.

The impact of trauma

As Daniella Kadene, a child psychotherapist, explains, most children will experience stress at some point in their lives, but not all stress affects them in the same way. Research distinguishes between everyday or short-term stress, such as meeting new people; stress that can feel overwhelming but manageable with support, such as a car accident; and more chronic stress that can exceed a child's ability to cope (Shonoff, 2009).

When experiences involve ongoing threat, fear or lack of safety, such as abuse or neglect, they are more likely to become traumatic. As Perry (2002) notes, trauma occurs when experiences fall outside what a child can psychologically manage and further intensifies when they are repeated or occur alongside other challenges such as poverty, instability or neglect (Walker *et al.*, 2011).

This isn't about pushing you towards your nearest therapist's door (for which I'll receive a commission of exactly zero). It's about providing you with awareness. After all, we can only ever change what we are aware of. For some of you, the trauma you've faced may feel like a distant memory or something you've buried deep, but while it may be blocked from your mind, it often lingers in your behaviours, decisions and relationships.

Due to some of the trauma I experienced as a child, there are entire years of my life that I can't fully remember. Certain memories feel blurry, distant, like they happened to someone else, or like I've only ever heard about them second-hand. I now understand that this is something called dissociation.

Dissociation is a psychological response to overwhelming stress or trauma. When something feels too painful, frightening or chaotic for the mind to process in the moment, it can 'switch off' to protect you. It's the brain's way of saying, 'This is too much right now – I'll deal with it later.' And for some of us, 'later' never really comes.

One of the most powerful moments during my therapy journey was when I was asked to reflect on my secondary school years. As I tried to piece those memories together, I realised I couldn't recall much of years 8 and 9, the time I was around 13 to 14 years old.

That just so happened to coincide with the period when my mum's partner lived with us and we experienced domestic abuse.

If you've ever felt like chunks of your past are missing, or like you were 'there but not there' during difficult times, you might've experienced dissociation too. It's more common than people think – and it's not a sign of weakness. It's your body's survival system doing what it has to do to keep you going. The healing comes when we slowly begin to reconnect with those parts of ourselves – not to relive the pain, but to understand it.

A word from Daniella Kadene, child psychotherapist

Daniella Kadene explains that dissociation is an adaptive survival strategy that allows a person to disconnect from their thoughts, feelings or experiences as a way of protecting themselves when there is no safe way to escape what is happening. For example, when a child is exposed to repeated traumatic experiences in which neither resistance nor escape feels possible, the mind may distance itself from reality in order to cope in the moment. This can involve 'zoning out', feeling numb or becoming detached from the experience, allowing the child to endure what would have otherwise felt overwhelming. Over time, this protective response can mean that parts of the experience are compartmentalised or not fully remembered.

Hearing this was both comforting and eye-opening; it gave me clarity about why those years felt like a blank space in my memory. However, while my mind had protected me by blocking out those events, my body, emotions and behaviours hadn't escaped. I had been carrying unresolved guilt, anger and frustration from that time without even realising it. Understanding this connection between past trauma and present behaviours has been transformative. It's helped me to stop operating on autopilot, driven by old wounds, and start parenting from a place of awareness, intention and healing.

Thinking about therapy?

Maybe you're someone who's been wondering about trying therapy for a while, but hasn't taken the leap yet. Or maybe you've already tried it and had either a positive or negative experience. Whatever your journey has been, I want to offer you this analogy: from the moment we are born we begin travelling through life with an invisible backpack strapped to our back. Every negative event or experience we face, whether it's trauma, heartbreak, disappointment or loss, becomes a small stone or brick added to that backpack. Over time, the weight builds. The older we get, the heavier that backpack becomes, often without us even realising it.

Now here's the important part: we have the opportunity to release some of this weight. By acknowledging these experiences, discussing them and working through the emotions they bring, we allow ourselves to remove some of those stones or bricks. In doing so, we lighten the load for the rest of our journey.

But it's not just our journey that's affected. This same backpack will, at some point, be shared with those closest to us – our child, our partner, our co-parent. Without even meaning to, we can pass those stones and bricks along through our behaviours, our reactions and the ways we show up (or fail to show up) for them. When we don't address what's in our backpack, we risk placing that weight on to the shoulders of the people we care about most.

REFLECTION: UNPACKING YOUR INVISIBLE BACKPACK

Take some time to think about that invisible backpack.

- Identify the stones or bricks. Write down a list of experiences or events that feel unresolved or continue to weigh on you.
- Acknowledge their impact. Reflect on how carrying these experiences has shaped the way you interact with others, especially your child or co-parent.
- Commit to lightening the load. Choose one stone or brick to address.

▶

Addressing a stone or brick doesn't have to be a dramatic moment for you – it can often be done quietly, calmly and with peace.

For some of you this may start with you simply admitting that something from your past still hurts or understanding that a reaction you often display has been shaped by something you experienced years ago.

For others, it might mean sitting with emotions you've been suppressing for years.

There is no single 'right' way to remove this weight from your backpack, but what matters most is your willingness to look inside it.

Every step you take to lighten your backpack not only helps you, it also ensures that your child and loved ones don't inherit the weight of your unprocessed experiences. Healing isn't just an individual journey, it's a gift we give to those we love.

Alternatives to therapy

I truly believe that every parent can benefit from therapy and, as a result, their child benefits, too. There's something deeply valuable about being able to sit in a space with someone who doesn't judge, who doesn't try to fix you or tell you what to do, but helps you understand your own thoughts.

For me, face-to-face therapy provided the rare chance to shut off from the noise of the world and just have an honest conversation with someone trained to hold space. That kind of support gave me clarity I didn't know I needed. But I also understand that therapy isn't always accessible, whether because of the cost, stigma or simply because it feels like too big a leap, especially if you've never done anything like it before.

My mum had been encouraging me to go to therapy for as long as I can remember, but I had to get there in my own time. I wasn't ready until I was ready – and maybe you're in that space right now, too. For this reason, I want to offer you some alternative tools that can help you reflect, heal and grow while you work out what's right for you:

Journalling

Getting your thoughts out of your system is often better than keeping them in. Writing freely about your feelings, memories and fears can help lighten your emotional load and prevent those emotions from spilling out on to others, especially in moments of anger or frustration.

Self-help books and audio resources

Books and podcasts offer reflections that are easy to access and digest in your own time. They're not a replacement for a therapist, but they can open your eyes to new perspectives.

Meaningful conversations

That said, I'd encourage you not to open up to too many people at once. Repeating the same story over and over can sometimes feel more draining than helpful. Instead, identify one or two people you trust deeply and lean on them when you need to. It's the quality of the support that matters, not the quantity.

Voice notes to self

It might sound strange, but for me this has often helped. I've found real value in simply talking out loud to myself, and recording voice notes on my phone has become a helpful outlet. It's private, honest and helps me process my emotions, especially when I can't quite write them down.

Nature walks and solitude

Sometimes, just stepping outside, walking in silence and giving your thoughts room to breathe can help you process things you didn't even know were sitting inside you. I find morning walks a great way to calm my mind and set my intentions for the day ahead. Nature tends to reflect what we need to hear without saying a word.

Spiritual or faith-based reflection

If you have a spiritual practice or connection to faith, then prayer, meditation or simply time in quiet reflection can bring a sense of peace, grounding and direction. It can also offer a community or belief system that holds you when you're struggling to hold yourself.

Apps and online tools

If you're looking for something more structured to guide your self-reflection, there are a number of apps designed to help.

None of these tools are meant to replace therapy, but they can help you start. They can keep you moving forward, even if it's just one step at a time. And when you're ready, I hope you allow yourself to take that next step towards therapy, too.

#38

Are you a good co-parent?

Growth requires reflection, which is why it's important to take moments to do exactly that, reflect – on your own behaviours. We've all had moments where emotions have got the better of us – trust me, I know. What I am about to ask you to do isn't to shame you or drown you in guilt, it's to help you grow, learn and do better for your child.

REFLECTION: SELF-ASSESSMENT EXERCISE

Take a few minutes to do this exercise, being completely honest.

- Think back to a moment where you felt…
  - Angry
  - Frustrated
  - Hurt
  - Disrespected
  - Let down by your co-parent
- Now ask yourself: did I react to that emotion instead of putting my child first? What was my reaction? Do any of the following apply?
  - I prevented my child from seeing the other parent.
  - I withheld or delayed money or financial support.
  - I ignored calls or messages about the child.
  - I said something about their other parent in front of them.

▶

* I used threats as a form of control.
* I made access or communication difficult on purpose.

- Think back to how that impacted your child. Was your child:
  * Caught in the middle?
  * Confused, upset or withdrawn?
  * Starting to copy your attitude towards the other parent?
  * Asking questions that made you uncomfortable?
  * Missing out on time, support or consistency?
- Now ask yourself honestly: have I become any of the 'difficult individuals' we previously spoke of? It's okay if the answer is yes. This is not about shame. This is your chance to own it, to change it.
- You can't change the past, but you can shape a better future for yourself and your child. Lastly, ask yourself: what can I do differently, moving forward?
- Write one small, intentional step you can take this week to:
  * Be more child-centred
  * Improve communication
  * Let go of the power struggle
  * Apologise if needed
  * Keep your child out of the emotional crossfire.

Part Four

Co-parenting ever after

#39

It's a date, not a playdate

This is one of the few moments in this book where I want the focus to shift completely on to you, not your child. Many parents enter the dating phase with their child at the forefront of every decision. And while I understand the intention behind that, because, yes, any serious partner will eventually be around your child, it's important to pause. Before you even think about the part of the journey where this individual meets your child, you need to make sure you're getting on the right bus.

Choosing the right partner starts with choosing what's right for you, not your child. Think about it: if this person becomes a long-term partner, they'll still be around years from now, when your child needs less from you, when you have more free time, when your child spends nights away, goes to college or university, or even starts a family of their own.

Now imagine if the person you committed to was chosen primarily because they seemed good for your child. Fast-forward to the future, when your child is grown and living their own life. You're now left with someone who was never actually compatible with you. In fact, you may realise you didn't fully know who you were as an individual when you chose them, because you were filtering everything through the lens of being a parent, not a person.

Seize the moment

Choosing a partner requires you to know yourself, your needs, your values and your desires, not just what you think will make things easier or better for your child. Dating is a moment for you to switch off and enjoy the company of someone else. Whether it's going on an actual date, a remote date, opening a dating app or agreeing to meet someone your friend Susan set you up with, at this point you're not committing to this person being around your child or moving in.

We often let our minds race ahead, imagining 10 steps down the road, and in doing so we miss the simple beauty of the evening, the conversation, the experience. Sometimes, that's exactly what we need.

For some, the idea of dating again might feel premature or even impossible, and that's completely fine. Others may have already declared that you won't even consider dating until your child is old enough to have grandchildren of their own. Wherever you stand, I aim to shed light on the pathway to dating again, especially for parents navigating this space after separation.

As a man with two amazing sons from two separate relationships, I can confidently say that if I had shut down the idea of dating again after my relationship with my eldest son's mum ended, I would have missed out on having my son Tyler.

Moving forward and embracing the possibility of love again as a parent is never easy, but it can be a beautiful journey that should be approached with thoughtfulness and care – and it's important to acknowledge that this experience differs significantly depending on whether you're the primary or non-resident parent.

Non-resident parents

The reality is your time is often less restricted. You may not have the same daily responsibilities or the constant demands of your child's routine. This gives you more 'child-free' time to explore the possibility of a new relationship. However, this doesn't mean the decision to date again comes without challenges or emotional considerations.

Primary parents

For you, the challenges can feel overwhelming. The lack of free time, the constant responsibilities, and the thought of introducing someone new into your child's life can make the prospect of dating seem impossible. Many parents feel it's easier and safer to decide they'll wait until their children are grown and independent before they even think about dating again.

On top of that, primary parents often wrestle with concerns about how a new partner might influence their child's life. Questions like, 'Will this person be a good role model?' or 'What happens if it doesn't work out?' can add layers of anxiety, making the whole idea feel like more trouble than it's worth.

The hope of reconciliation

For some of you there might still be a lingering hope of reconciling with your child's other parent. While some might scoff at the idea with an emphatic 'Absolutely not!', it's worth acknowledging that this hope, whether realistic or not, can also delay your decision to move forward and explore new relationships (for more on this *see* pp. 213–214).

The positives of dating

Although there are so many social media vampires who do their best to put fear in the hearts of single parents when it comes to dating and the risks of having the wrong person around your child, let's touch on something that they won't ever highlight – the positives!

Since Tyler was born I've had three relationships, the longest lasting four years. None of them became lifelong partnerships. Could that be seen as a failure? Perhaps. Some might even say it's too many new people for my children to have had to get to know. I'm sure there are those who hold that view, but I wouldn't change a thing, because each relationship taught me valuable lessons and shaped the man I am today.

I've grown, reflected and learned more about myself in ways I wouldn't have without those experiences. Importantly, my children met incredible individuals along the way, all of whom showed them nothing but love and care. Those connections, even if temporary, were meaningful.

Tyler's mum was also in a dating phase at one point, before meeting her now-husband and Tyler's stepfather. Seeing her this happy and truly fulfilled is something I genuinely celebrate. She's now with a man who meets not just her wants but her needs, and that makes all the difference, because my son gets to see his mum happy and is being raised in an environment that reflects that, which is ultimately what matters most to me.

#40

Dating yourself first

I was once asked on social media, 'What do you wish your mum had done differently?' My response was simple: 'I wish my mum had poured more into her own cup than just mine.' Reflecting on her journey, I realise I didn't see enough moments when she was over the moon, beaming with joy or simply living for herself. She dedicated so much of her time to being a mum that she forgot motherhood was just one role she was blessed with and it was never meant to erase the person she was or eliminate her need for happiness.

Finding joy in your life – be it nights out with friends, solo trips, spa breaks, playing pool with the guys, even dating – teaches your child the invaluable lesson that happiness and fulfilment are essential for everyone, including parents.

Now some of you may not have the biggest social circles, friends who also share the same interests, or a partner who is willing to tag along to events, but that should never be a reason for you to delay your happiness or miss out on creating memories that you are deserving of. So here's a concept I want you to think about: dating yourself. 'Huh?' you might say. But yes, you read that correctly. I mean think about it, who better to treat you right than you?

Dating yourself can be a great starting point before you date anyone else. It's something I've started doing and I genuinely look forward to it. Dating yourself will look different for everyone, but at its core it's a moment to tune in and truly listen to what you enjoy. It's giving yourself permission to do the things you want to do without waiting for others, without worrying if someone else is as excited as you are and without diluting your experience to make it more comfortable for someone else. It's a chance to be fully present with yourself.

Who are you?

Start by writing a list of all the things you've been wanting to experience: the movies you want to watch, the theatre shows or concerts you'd love to attend, the restaurants you've been meaning to try, the places you'd love to visit. Once you have that list, choose one thing and go for it, alone.

Book the ticket. Don't overthink it. Just pick one, get ready, choose an outfit that makes you feel good and step out to enjoy being you. Whether it's getting your hair done or, if you're like me, appreciating the freedom of not having to worry about that part, use this moment to show up for yourself with intention. Once you start, you'll realise how empowering it feels, because being alone doesn't mean being lonely. It means valuing your own company enough to honour your desires before those of anyone else.

These moments help you figure out what you like and dislike, and they give you space to connect with yourself. The more you understand who you are, the clearer it becomes what type of partner would suit you.

What do you like? Dislike? What makes you laugh? What's your favourite place to eat? How do you like to switch off? What's on your bucket list? Do you even have a bucket list? I'm not asking to overwhelm you, but rather to remind you that so many of us lose sight of ourselves in the chaos of life. Taking time for yourself can help you rediscover the person you were before life got busy. The more you understand what makes you tick, the clearer it becomes what kind of partner would truly align with your needs and desires.

Reconnect with you, because that's the foundation for everything else. For some of you, you may have lost touch with who you are, as you have now become someone who believes their sole purpose is to cater to another individual. Remember, you were someone before this child and it's so important to never lose sight of that person. No matter how amazing a parent you are, it is only a role you play, it is not who you are.

Go it alone

Sometimes, we feel life can only be experienced with others, which leads to loneliness or rushing into relationships to fill a void. After years of missing out on concerts and events because I didn't have a date, I decided to stop waiting for someone to join me. I started buying two tickets to events I wanted to attend, then figuring out who was coming, which would usually be my best friend, Oz. She'll tag along to anything that gets her out of the house, no questions asked. I pray everyone has an Oz in their life.

I remember going to see Daughtry at the Royal Albert Hall. I bought one ticket and the experience was so freeing. I left when I was ready, didn't stress about being late or whether anyone else was enjoying the show, and was fully present. I didn't even pull out my phone as much as usual. I was just in the moment.

I also remember seeing *Creed* with Michael B. Jordan when it first came out. To this day, it's my favourite cinema experience. There was something peaceful about being on my own, not worrying about anyone else's experience. It was so good I made it a tradition to see every new *Creed* movie by myself.

The point I'm making is that dating again is about you. It's a chance to enjoy yourself and take a well-deserved break from parenthood; to be someone who isn't responsible for anyone else for a short while. So why wouldn't you welcome this opportunity again? I'm not here to persuade you, but to open your mind to the possibilities.

Remember that you are in control and you get to decide when to start dating again. Doing it isn't a way to cope with the end of a previous relationship or something you do because friends and family are encouraging you to 'move on with your life'. You are not dating because you are lonely; you are dating because you are ready.

REFLECTION: TIME TO LOOK AFTER YOU

Take 15 minutes today and answer this question honestly:

- What parts of myself have I neglected while pouring into others?

Then ask yourself:

- When was the last time I did something just for me?
- What does happiness look like outside of parenting?
- When did my child last see me laughing, rested, free?

Now write down one small thing you'll do this week for you – not as a parent, not as a partner, not for anyone else; just for you.

Because you matter.

And when you're whole, they get the best of you.

Not just what's left of you.

#41

Closing the door on reconciliation

Before you step into anything new, make sure you've closed any loose ends from previous relationships. If there are lingering conversations you've avoided, unresolved feelings you've buried or a lack of transparency with someone from your past they will eventually surface and it will make building something new much harder.

I say this from experience. I've been the guy who entered a new relationship, only to realise the bond between my partner and her co-parent wasn't as finished as I had believed. It created tension, uncertainty, a space where no relationship could truly grow – and ultimately it didn't. Learn from my mistakes. Clear your past, be honest with yourself, and give your future relationships the fresh start they deserve.

Sometimes, we avoid difficult conversations, because in the moment it feels easier. But in the long run, what we avoid now can grow into a much bigger issue later, risking the calm and cooperative co-parenting relationship you've worked hard to build. If you truly want to move forward and step through new doors that serve you better, you must be willing to fully close the ones that no longer do.

Think about it like this: our cars are built with warning systems that alert us if a door is still open when we try to drive off. Why? Because leaving a door open while moving puts not just the driver, but everyone inside, including our child, at risk. Relationships are similar. The only difference is, when it comes to emotional doors you don't get a flashing light warning you that something is still open.

This doesn't mean you need to have a dramatic conversation every time you speak to your co-parent, especially if you're simply discussing pick-up times or school events. But if conversations about reconciliation ever come up, it's important not to send mixed signals.

You don't have to be harsh and say, 'There's no chance of us ever being together again', but you do need to make your position clear, with kindness and firmness, so there's no room for confusion. Clarity protects you, your co-parent and, most importantly, your child, from unnecessary emotional turmoil down the line.

#42

The right partner for you

The truth is, being 'ready' to start dating again doesn't usually come with a big flashing sign or a perfect checklist. It's more of a feeling, a shift inside you. It's when dating starts to feel like an opportunity, not a chore. When the idea of meeting someone new brings a sense of curiosity and excitement, rather than pressure and dread.

You might still feel a few nerves, and that's normal. It's natural to feel a little uncertain or cautious, but underneath those nerves there's a quiet confidence. You feel settled enough within yourself to know that you can invite someone into your world without losing who you are. You're not looking for someone to fix you or complete you; you're simply open to sharing the life you've built.

Now, life isn't always light and easy. Responsibilities, past hurts and everyday pressures can make it hard to feel completely settled. That's okay. Being ready doesn't mean you have everything perfectly figured out, but you're aware of your purpose for dating. Whether it's to connect, to learn, to grow or to share joy with someone new, you understand why you're opening yourself up again.

You're not chasing validation. You're not trying to fill a gap. You're choosing to date because you're excited about the possibility of building something meaningful, whether that's a friendship, a partnership, or simply experiencing new moments with someone who adds light to your journey.

If you can approach dating with a sense of hope instead of heaviness, if you look forward to the process more than you fear it, you're probably ready. And remember, you're allowed to enjoy it. You're allowed to feel good about wanting companionship and entering this new chapter of life.

Wants and needs – understanding the difference

If you don't know the difference between what you want and what you need in a relationship then you'll constantly find yourself feeling unfulfilled, even when you get everything you thought you asked for. Wants and needs are not the same thing, and understanding the difference is crucial if you want to build a relationship that actually lasts.

Wants are the things we desire – the nice-to-haves that can make a relationship feel even better, but aren't essential for it to survive. Think of it like furnishing a home: you might want a huge TV or a designer sofa, but the home itself can still be lived in without them. They add to the experience, but they're not the foundation.

A personal want for me is having a partner who enjoys R&B music as much as I do. It would be incredible to share that passion, vibe to the same playlists and enjoy concerts together. But if they didn't love R&B, it wouldn't break the relationship. It's a preference, not a deal-breaker.

Needs, however, are non-negotiable. They're the foundation, the walls, the roof of that home. Without them, everything eventually collapses. In the context of music, a need for me would be having a partner who accepts and respects my love for R&B, even if it's not their thing. I need the freedom to play my music without feeling judged or made to feel like it's a problem.

Another example: through experience, I've learned that I need a partner who is supportive of the work I do. I don't need them to actively help, or even fully understand every detail, but I do need them to recognise its importance to me and respect the time, passion and commitment it demands. If someone belittles or resents what drives me, that's not just a clash of interests – it's a fundamental misalignment.

Recognising the difference between wants and needs helps you make healthier choices when dating. It stops you from compromising on the things that actually matter to your well-being and keeps you grounded when the surface-level stuff – the hobbies, the aesthetics, the dream vacations – eventually fade into the background.

Wants are the extras. Needs are the essentials. Knowing which is which could be the difference between a relationship that feels good for a season and one that feels right for a lifetime. Here's a simple checklist of some common wants and needs that people often confuse, showing how easily we sometimes prioritise the wrong things without realising it:

Wants (nice to have, but not essential)
These are bonuses – they add flavour, but aren't the foundation:

- Similar music taste
- Shared hobbies (you both love hiking, gaming or travelling)
- Physical appearance preferences (height, body type, hairstyle)
- Fashion sense or personal style
- Financial status beyond stability (being wealthy rather than just financially responsible)
- Big romantic gestures (flowers, gifts, surprises)
- A particular career or job title.

Needs (essential for a healthy, lasting relationship)
These are non-negotiables – without them, the relationship will crack:

- Respect for your passions, values and individuality
- Emotional availability and willingness to communicate
- Shared core values (views on trust, family, loyalty)
- Consistent honesty and transparency
- Support for your personal growth (not holding you back)
- Ability to resolve conflict in a healthy way (no silent treatment or explosions)
- Willingness to compromise and adapt when needed
- Respect for boundaries (both yours and their own).

Ask yourself: would the relationship be emotionally and mentally unsafe, unstable or unfulfilling without it? If the answer is yes, it's a need. If it's no, it's a want.

REFLECTION: WHAT DO YOU WANT IN A PARTNER – AND WHAT DO YOU NEED?

This exercise will help you gain clarity on the difference between what you desire in a partner and what you truly need for a fulfilling, healthy relationship.

On a piece of paper or even in your phone notebook, divide the page into two columns and create two lists:

Wants

- What qualities would be nice for your partner to have, but aren't essential for the relationship to work?
  Think about shared hobbies, personality traits or lifestyle preferences (loves to travel, enjoys R&B music, has a great sense of humour).

Needs

- What qualities are essential for you to feel respected, valued and secure in the relationship?
  These may include values, communication styles, emotional support or lifestyle agreements (respects my work, values family time, can communicate openly).

Ask yourself these questions

- How would I feel without this want being met?
- Would the relationship still be capable of thriving without this?
- What happens if this need is not met? Would I feel compromised or diminished in any way?

▶

Refine your list

- Highlight the top three non-negotiable needs and the top three desires.
  Was there anything that surprised you about your wants versus your needs?

Although I've emphasised the importance of dating for you, it's worth noting that this journey can also have a positive impact on your child. By simply enjoying the process – not necessarily finding a partner right away, but embracing the experience – you may begin to feel lighter, happier and more fulfilled. That joy naturally radiates to your child, who will sense that energy and witness someone they truly adore being happy.

Every child, whether they can articulate it or not, wants that for their parent. As they grow older, they're more likely to look back and say, 'I'm glad my mum/dad was happy' rather than feeling the weight of knowing their parent missed out on the possibility of finding love because they prioritised parenting above all else. That's not a burden any child should carry.

#43

Telling your co-parent you're dating again

Informing your co-parent that you've decided to start dating again is a personal decision, but one that requires careful thought, because every co-parenting dynamic is different. Some co-parents may react respectfully, while others may become spiteful, controlling or change their behaviour in ways that add unnecessary stress. And that's the last thing you need in the early stages of getting to know someone new.

You are only ever responsible for how you act and react, never for how someone else behaves, so with that in mind, I would usually advise that if the person you're dating becomes someone you can genuinely see meeting your child, that's a good point to inform your co-parent.

The reason is simple: if your child meets someone new and your co-parent hasn't been informed, it may put your child in a difficult position. They may feel they need to stay silent to avoid being questioned or they may mention it naturally and still be quizzed. Our aim is always to protect our child, not place them in the middle of adult decisions.

However, it's important to acknowledge that not every co-parenting set-up is safe or healthy. Some parents may choose not to disclose their dating life because of safeguarding concerns, especially if sharing that information could lead to conflict, manipulation or emotional harm. If this applies to you, your priority must always be your child's well-being and your own safety.

Informing your co-parent that you are dating again while there is no involvement with your child, is not a conversation I believe is necessary and it's one that can take away from you enjoying the experience of getting to know someone new.

A friend of mine, who shall remain nameless, but for the purposes of this story let's call him Kevin, had convinced us all that he was well beyond the relationship with his co-parent and had even began dating women again, of which his co-parent was aware. Someone within the group then spotted Kevin's co-parent on a dating app and casually let him know. His reaction caught us all off guard and was very hypocritical. Reminding him that the emotion he was feeling was his ego and that his co-parent was entitled to move on, just like he had been doing, eventually calmed him down.

Even if enough time has passed between you and your co-parent's relationship ending, they may still show signs of jealousy, become overly inquisitive, or start challenging decisions they previously left alone. Seeing you move on or being happy with someone new can stir emotions they didn't expect to feel, like insecurity, regret or resentment.

It's important to understand that *their reaction isn't your responsibility to manage, but your response is.* You don't need to argue, explain or justify your decision to start dating again. What you do need is to stay grounded, respectful and focused on your child. It helps to be clear on a few things:

- **You're allowed to move on:** As long as your decisions aren't putting your child at risk, who you choose to see in your personal time isn't something your co-parent gets to control.
- **Be firm but fair with boundaries:** If your co-parent is overstepping the mark or trying to guilt-trip you, it's okay to say, 'I respect that this might be hard for you, but this is my personal life. It doesn't involve our child's well-being and I'd prefer we stay focused on co-parenting.'

- **Avoid tit-for-tat dynamics:** Just because they dated first or brought someone new around quickly doesn't mean you have to. And just because they're reacting poorly doesn't mean you need to retaliate. Take the high road, because it benefits your child in the long run.
- **Don't use your new relationship as a weapon:** No matter how tempting it might be, avoid throwing your happiness in their face or parading your new partner to provoke a reaction. This only adds fuel to an already emotional situation.
- **Prepare for shifts:** Sometimes, dating can change the dynamic between you and your co-parent. They may pull away, become colder or less cooperative. This is where maturity matters. Continue being consistent, clear and committed to your shared responsibilities.

Your co-parent's reaction might say more about where they are emotionally than it does about your choices. You can't control how they feel, but you can choose not to get pulled into unnecessary conflict. Keep your focus on peace, on protecting your child's emotional environment and on choosing relationships that actually add to your life. If dating someone new threatens your co-parent's ego, that's their issue to work through, not your cross to carry.

Remember this: informing your co-parent is not about seeking their permission or approval. You do not need either. It's simply an act of respect and an effort to maintain a calm environment for your child and ensure they never become the messenger or the one caught in the middle.

#44

When to introduce a new partner

A quick Google search on 'when to introduce a new partner to your child' will yield countless articles and opinions. The same goes for social media, where everyone seems to have a perspective, even those who have never been parents, let alone separated parents.

The truth is, if you introduced someone to your child after a week and that relationship led to a marriage lasting 30 years, no one would have a negative thing to say. But if that same relationship ended after a month, you'd suddenly be labelled a bad parent for introducing someone too soon.

People rarely have opinions until things go wrong, but that's life. Here's the good news, though: you're not living your life for anyone else. When it comes to introducing someone new to your child, you are the best person to make that call. You know your child best and understand the dynamics of your relationship better than anyone else.

Of course, it's wise to be comfortable and confident in who you're dating before bringing them into your child's life. But just like a first date, an introduction doesn't mean this person is here to stay or that your child will immediately see them as a step-parent.

In fact, introductions can be valuable opportunities to see how your child and partner interact. I've seen situations where people waited years before introducing their partner, only to discover they didn't connect well with the child, ultimately leading to a break-up. That's a valuable insight they could've gained much sooner.

I once waited a year for a previous partner to meet my child and, guess what, that relationship didn't last, but on the other hand Tyler met his mum's partner, who is now his stepdad, much sooner than the 'wait a year' fan club would recommend, and now they're happily married and thriving as a blended family. Every situation is unique. Trust yourself to know what's right for your family.

One important thing to keep in mind is that non-resident parents often have more free time away from their child. This can allow them to develop a stronger bond with a new partner much sooner than a primary parent, who may be balancing parenting responsibilities alone and only has the occasional free evening to date.

Because of this, some parents may feel pressured to rush the process of introducing their child to a new partner, hoping it will make it easier to spend time with that person or incorporate them into their home life. My advice? Don't rush this process. It's essential that both you and your child are ready for this introduction. When handled thoughtfully, it can pave the way for a positive dynamic. If done too soon, it can cause confusion or discomfort for your child.

Your new partner should never push for the introduction. They should respect your timeline and be supportive of going at a pace that feels right for you and your child. That said, if your relationship is serious and heading towards long-term commitment, it's understandable that they may not want to wait indefinitely. Finding the balance is key. When handled with care, this transition can become a natural and meaningful step forward for everyone involved.

Picking the right moment

So, you've met someone special and are contemplating introducing them to your child. First of all, congratulations! This is a significant step and can feel overwhelming as you navigate the desire to do things right.

The fact that you're being thoughtful about this is already a great sign as it shows you're prioritising your child's well-being, which is exactly what any good parent would do. Trust yourself and find comfort in your careful approach.

What follows isn't meant to push you in any particular direction or tell you exactly what to do. Instead, it's here to offer insights that might help as you make the decision that's best for your family.

How long ago was the break-up?

Each of your situations will be unique. Some of you may have never been in a serious relationship with your co-parent, while others may have recently gone through a divorce. Some might be co-parenting with children in primary school or beyond, while others may have separated when your child was still an infant.

Neither of my children experienced a sustained period of time where their mums and I were together, as we separated early in their lives. As a result, they never had to process a break-up or significant change in circumstances; they simply grew up in the environment they've always known. The point is, there's no one-size-fits-all solution here. Every family dynamic is different, and that's something no one can truly understand unless they're in your shoes.

For younger children, the process of meeting your new partner may be a little smoother, especially if they've never known you and their other parent together or aren't old enough to fully grasp the situation. On the other hand, if you're dealing with older children, you may want to take things slower, as they might still be processing the separation or divorce. Being mindful of where your child is emotionally will help guide your approach.

If there has been a recent break-up and your child is old enough to understand and process the situation, it might be helpful to have age-appropriate conversations about you and your co-parent moving on. The goal here isn't to give your child the power to make decisions for you, but rather to make them feel included and informed about what's happening. You may be surprised by their responses.

This doesn't mean sitting them down for a heavy, emotional announcement. It means creating a safe space for honest but simple explanations that meet them where they are developmentally. Children, much like adults, often worry about how change will affect them personally – their routines, their sense of stability, and their relationship with each parent. When handled with care, early conversations can help reduce anxiety, prevent misunderstandings, and give them the emotional tools they need to adjust.

I remember having a conversation with Tyler when he was around eight years old about me finding a partner, and he mentioned that he didn't think it was fair that his mum was married while I was still single. He told me he wanted me to have someone, too. Hearing this from him was actually quite refreshing and encouraging. It reminded me that, deep down, children want the best for us, even if they don't always have the words to fully express it. I share this with you because it's a reminder that children can be more understanding and compassionate than we sometimes expect.

And starting the conversation doesn't need to be complicated. You might simply ask your child what they think about you spending time with someone new or how they would feel if you were to meet a partner in the future. Their response will often give you a good sense of their emotional readiness. Depending on their age, you can also gently reassure them with simple truths that offer comfort and clarity like:

- Families can look different and that's okay.
- Sometimes, adults realise they're better parents when they live in different homes.
- No matter what changes, I'm still your mum/dad and that will never change.

These small reminders can go a long way in helping your child feel secure during times of change. They reinforce stability without overwhelming them with too many details. The goal isn't to convince your child of anything, it's to create an open, honest space where they feel included, considered and safe.

The honeymoon phase can be just that

We've all experienced it – that intoxicating thrill at the beginning of a relationship when everything feels exciting and perfect. The honeymoon phase can be one of the best parts of a relationship, because it delivers that dopamine hit, making us crave more time and connection with the person.

Interestingly, a 2020 study published in *Frontiers in Psychology* found that early feelings of love are fuelled by brain regions rich in dopamine and oxytocin, our brain's 'feel-good' chemicals that sustain romantic connection. While there's no set timeline, a 2015 study from

New York University found this phase can last up to 24 months. Now I'm not suggesting you wait two and a half years before introducing someone to your child, but it's helpful to recognise that these early feelings don't always provide the clarity needed for long-term decisions. Look beyond the thrill and ask yourself if this relationship is truly built on a solid foundation.

Check your motives

Consider why you're thinking about this introduction. Is this someone you see as a potential spouse or long-term partner, or is this simply a fun, casual relationship? There's no wrong answer here, but if it's the latter it might be worth keeping this relationship separate from your child for now to avoid unnecessary attachment.

If you see a future with this person, it's important to ensure you're on the same page. Have honest, transparent conversations to make sure your partner shares similar long-term goals, especially if you're considering involving your child.

Involve the other parent (if possible)

If your co-parenting dynamic allows for this then I'm a strong advocate for communicating with the other parent about your new partner and your desire for them to meet your child – but only if discussing this with them won't lead to unnecessary drama. Now, you don't need their permission, but showing consideration can set a positive tone.

You might even arrange for a brief, informal introduction between your new partner and the other parent. This doesn't have to be a formal meeting, even a simple 'hi and bye' can help foster transparency.

In the past I had unrealistic expectations, believing my child's mum should never introduce anyone new to our son. That mindset was controlling and rooted in fear. Because I didn't create an open environment, she likely didn't feel comfortable telling me when someone new entered their lives.

As a result, I learned about a new partner through our son. I found myself questioning my five-year-old endlessly about this man. Looking back, that was unfair to my child. Did I meet this man? No. Did he stay?

No. Did he cause harm? No. But did my fear lead me to place my child in an uncomfortable position, potentially affecting our relationship? Yes. In moments like these, always ask yourself: do my actions truly support the best interests of my child?

No matter how many new partners your co-parent chooses to date or bring into contact with your child, the only one who can impact your relationship with your child is you. The only one responsible for that relationship is you. So focus on nurturing that bond and not on what the other parent is doing in their own relationships.

Over time, I learned to trust that my child's mum, like me, only wants what's best for our child. We chose each other to be parents for a reason. Neither of us would ever intentionally bring harm to our child. That understanding has brought me peace when new partners were introduced in later years.

The main point I want you to take from all this is that there is never a rush, there is never a right time, there is never a perfect way and that's why I want you to trust your instincts. Be thoughtful and intentional. And remember, this is your journey, and you are the best person to make the right decision for you and your child.

#45

Handling the introductions

You've carefully weighed the pros and cons, done all the overthinking your mind can handle, maybe even asked everyone in your circle, and you've finally made the decision that you'd like your child to meet your partner.

At this stage, it's important to remember that children meet new people all the time. Whether it's teachers, family friends, coaches or the parents of their friends, new faces are a part of their everyday lives, so in many ways this isn't as unusual for them as it might seem.

Rather than thinking of it as introducing your child to someone who might play a significant role in their future, try framing it as simply introducing a new friend of yours. Now, I'm not saying it's always that simple. My eldest, Omari, didn't waste any time recognising that the woman he was meeting at 16 was his dad's new partner. Meanwhile, Tyler, who was 10 at the time, could easily be convinced that this was just 'Daddy's friend'. After all, he still believed in the tooth fairy and Father Christmas, so persuading him didn't take much work!

Keep in mind that your child's perception and understanding of the situation will vary based on their age and maturity level, so approach the introduction in a way that feels comfortable for both you and them.

Choosing the right location

When it comes to introducing your child to your new partner, it's important to make the experience enjoyable for everyone involved. It doesn't have to be anything fancy or expensive, but it's a good idea to choose a neutral, low-pressure location where everyone can feel comfortable. Some good options include:

- A park
- The zoo
- A bowling alley
- A family party or event
- Mini golf
- Or an activity based on your child's interests.

The goal is to create a relaxed environment where the interaction feels natural, without overwhelming the child with an unfamiliar setting. This helps ensure that the first meeting goes smoothly and everyone can enjoy the experience without feeling too much pressure. You might even want to consider inviting a small group of friends along so the focus isn't solely on the introduction, which can help your child feel more at ease.

Remember, this first meet-up is just an introduction, not a test. You're there to see how they interact and how everyone feels. There's no need to make it a big event or put any pressure on how it should unfold. Just enjoy the moment.

To your child this is simply a fun day out with their parent and some friends or a normal family party. Nothing out of the ordinary needs to be highlighted and it doesn't need to be turned into a big deal.

In a past relationship, my partner at the time had children around the same age as my boys. We decided that it would be nice for us to first meet each other's children one-on-one, without the other kids present. We later brought all the children together.

This approach worked well for us, but it's by no means a requirement. Sometimes, it's helpful to see that one-on-one interaction first to get a sense of how things will go, rather than managing multiple kids at once, but you should do what feels right for you and your situation.

Debriefing after the initial meeting

After that first get-together, I personally think it's crucial to take a moment to debrief with both your child and your partner. Check in with everyone involved, including yourself, to see how everyone felt about the experience. Ask yourself: did it feel right? How did it compare with what I expected? Were there any surprises, positive or negative, that stood out?

This reflection is important, because it helps you process how the introduction went and gives you the opportunity to address any concerns, big or small. If the meeting went well, this debriefing could also create positive momentum, helping you feel more confident as you move forward with planning future interactions. Additionally, the conversation can help you gauge how comfortable your child and partner are with each other, and whether there's anything that needs to be adjusted before the next step.

It's a valuable chance to reflect on what worked and what might need tweaking. This isn't about perfection, but rather about ensuring that everyone is moving at a speed that feels right for them. Remember, there's no rush. This is just one step in a bigger process of building healthy relationships, so trust your instincts and be open to adjusting as you go along. The goal is to create a comfortable and positive environment for both your child and your partner, allowing them both to build a connection at their own pace.

REFLECTION: TRUSTING YOURSELF THROUGH THE INTRODUCTION PROCESS

Introducing a new partner to your child is not a moment to take lightly, but it also doesn't need to be clouded by fear, judgement or unrealistic expectations. This task can be used as a checklist to help you reflect on your unique situation, build clarity around your decision-making process, and move forward with confidence. Take your time and answer the following prompts:

Looking back

- How long has it been since your last relationship ended?
- Have you and your child had time to emotionally process the separation (if necessary)?
- Is your child familiar with the idea that you may meet someone new?

Understanding your why

- What are your motivations for introducing this partner now?
- Are you looking to validate your relationship, simplify your life or truly begin blending your family?

Beyond the honeymoon

- Are you still in the early stages of the relationship or have you had enough time to see this person through a range of real-life situations?

Considering your child's perspective

- How do you think your child might feel about meeting someone new?
- Have you spoken with them in an age-appropriate way about the idea of you dating?
- What might they need from you to feel safe and reassured?

The other parent's involvement

- Is it realistic or helpful to inform your co-parent about this introduction?
- Would a quick introduction between your partner and co-parent help ease future tensions?

Logistics and planning

- Have you thought about where the introduction will take place?

▶

- What kind of setting would feel relaxed, neutral, and pressure-free?

Now that you've taken time to reflect, sit with your answers before making any final decisions.

Introductions don't require perfection, only thoughtfulness and a child-centred mindset. Whether this meeting happens next week or next year, your intention to do right by your child will always be the most important part.

#46

Understanding blended families

At its core, a blended family is the coming together of individuals often from previous relationships to form a new household or unit of care and connection. It doesn't require marriage. It doesn't require a formal contract. It's about intentional living, about creating a space where children feel safe, seen and supported, no matter whose blood runs in their veins.

Now the phrase 'blended family' can stir up a whole mix of emotions – comfort, confusion, hope, fear, frustration or even anger – depending on where you are in your journey. And the truth is, not everyone is ready, willing or even interested in blending families. That's okay. As I always say, there is no one-size-fits-all approach to co-parenting and this book isn't about forcing you into ideas you're not prepared for. It's about helping you understand yourself, your boundaries, your emotions and ultimately what is best for you and your child.

Right now, you might not be in a place where the idea of blending families feels possible or even tolerable. If that's you, I want to gently encourage you not to lock the door on the idea permanently but maybe just keep it ajar for now, because growth can move us into rooms we once swore we'd never enter.

I say this because I've been there. The idea of my child's mum ever blending a family with another man used to send what felt like electric currents through my body, filling me with anger, jealousy and insecurity all at once. I hated the thought of it.

Looking back, I can see that my reaction had everything to do with where I was on my journey and nothing to do with what was best for my child. My mindset was focused on me, my ego, my fears and what I thought I would be losing, not my child's well-being. At the time, I saw blending families as:

- Another man living in the same household as my child and 'replacing' me
- My child calling someone else 'Dad'.

All these fears were emotional responses to wounds I hadn't addressed and insecurities I hadn't yet confronted. I saw blending a family as defeat for the one I first created. I saw it as something rare and negative, but I was so wrong.

Blended families are a growing part of modern parenting, yet they're often left out of the conversation. In the UK, in 2021, there were over three-quarters of a million stepfamilies and most included dependent children. The majority of step-parents were men, and many of these families involved both biological and stepchildren living under one roof. Around one in 11 children were living in stepfamilies and they were 3.5 times more likely to live in a cohabiting couple family (48.6%) than those living in non-stepfamilies.

These stats are a reflection of where modern-day parenting currently stands. They serve as a reminder that not only do relationships fail and end, but new ones can be formed that uplift, support and benefit us and our children, as long as we are open to the idea.

Are you hesitant or fearful?

If the idea of a blended family feels too difficult, you're not alone. It's okay to feel unsure. It's okay to have questions or doubts. Many people wrestle with fears of losing control, being replaced or repeating old mistakes. But know this: a new chapter for you or your co-parent doesn't erase your role in your child's story. It doesn't diminish your love or importance. In fact, by supporting a healthy blended dynamic you increase the security and happiness your child experiences.

And to those who've sworn never to accept a blended set-up, please pause and reflect. Is that belief rooted in protection or in pride?

Are you afraid of your child being harmed or of your ego being bruised? These are the hard questions you must ask yourself if you truly want to put your child first.

Facing my own fears

Through therapy, reflection and growth, I've come to understand a difficult truth: I used to believe that once you had a child with someone, there was a kind of unspoken bond that meant that person was somehow 'yours' forever. In my mind, impregnating someone felt more significant than marriage; it felt final.

But that was a warped, possessive and ultimately unhelpful mindset. The reality is that you are not tied to your child's other parent – you are tied to the child. That is where your focus, energy and responsibility should lie.

I feared that if my child's mother moved on, it meant my role was being replaced or, worse, erased. I imagined a scenario where another man would become more important, where my place in my child's life would diminish. But here's what I now need every co-parent – especially fathers – to understand:

> The presence of another adult in your child's life does not erase you.

I remember the first time I met Tyler's mum's partner, now his stepfather. It was at one of Tyler's football sessions when he was around three years old. We both ended up sitting on the sidelines, watching Tyler play.

That day we had a genuine conversation, just two men talking, not as rivals, but as people who cared deeply about the same child. He shared a bit about his own co-parenting experience and it became clear that he understood the value of respect in situations like ours.

Knowing he had navigated a co-parenting dynamic himself reassured me. It showed me that he understood his role and had no intention of stepping into mine. He was respectful, calm and clear that he wasn't there to replace me as Tyler's father.

And that's something I believe every parent hopes to hear when someone new enters their child's life – that they recognise and respect the existing bond between parent and child. That moment gave me peace, and it set the tone for what would grow into a healthy blended family dynamic.

Today, my child's mother has been married for over six years. They each came into the relationship with a child and have since gone on to create two more beautiful children together. They are the living, breathing definition of a blended family. And rather than feel threatened by that, I've learned to see it as something powerful and possible for even myself.

Blended families come in many forms. For some it means both partners already have children and choose not to have more. For others only one person may bring a child into the relationship. Some couples go on to have children together, while others focus solely on building harmony between those already in the picture. There's no rulebook – only respect, patience and mutual understanding.

You don't need to wait for perfection to begin again. Blending a family isn't about getting everything right, it's about showing up with love and the willingness to grow together. You have the power to build something beautiful. Not just for yourself, but for the child watching you. So whether you're on the outside looking in, thinking 'I could never do that,' or you're standing at the edge, wondering if it's possible for you, too, know this:

> It can work.
>
> It does work.
>
> And it might just be the second chance at love and family that you need.

The potential power of blended families

When approached with the right mindset, blended families can offer children a wider circle of love: more people cheering them on at school events, more people to lean on when life gets tough, more models of healthy relationships, teamwork and compromise. When done well, a blended family expands rather than replaces their world. Children in blended families can learn:

- That love can exist in different forms and still be real
- That cooperation and mutual respect between adults, even those who once were in conflict, is possible
- That family isn't always about who you share DNA with, but who shows up for you when it matters most.

Things to consider before you blend

Blending a family is not a decision to take lightly. It comes with its own challenges, emotions and growing pains for both the adults and the children involved. Before moving in together or beginning to co-raise children, ask yourself:

- Are we both emotionally ready to take this step?
- Have we had honest conversations about parenting styles, roles and boundaries?
- Are we committed to working through inevitable conflict with respect and patience?
- Have we taken the time to help the child involved feel heard, safe and prepared?

Just because you love someone doesn't automatically mean you're ready to raise children together, especially when one or both of you already have them. Blending requires more than romance. It demands maturity, empathy and intentionality.

#47

Blended family challenges

One of the biggest hurdles for blended families is figuring out everyone's new role. Unlike traditional families, where who does what is often clearer, blended families can face confusion. It's not always obvious how everyone should treat or relate to each other, especially when a new adult, usually a step-parent, joins the picture.

For step-parents, this can be especially tricky. They might feel they are expected to act like a parent, but don't want to come on too strong. At the same time, children may struggle with accepting a step-parent's role, particularly if it feels like that person is replacing their biological parent. This can cause tension, especially in the early days of the new family set-up.

Solutions for happier, healthier blended families

It doesn't have to stay that way, though. Here are some solutions to help the whole family adjust and keep the child's well-being at the heart of it all:

Take it slow

Step-parents don't have to rush into a parenting role. Start by building trust and connection through small, consistent acts of care. Play games, show an interest in their hobbies or simply listen.

Communicate openly and often

Have honest conversations about expectations. Adults should discuss their roles clearly and privately, then gently share age-appropriate ideas with the child.

Respect existing bonds

Don't try to replace the other parent. Encourage children to maintain a healthy relationship with both biological parents if it's safe and possible.

Work as a team

Biological parents should support step-parents by backing them up and helping define what their role should be. Show a united front when it comes to rules and routines.

Set clear, shared boundaries

Children feel safer when everyone knows the rules and sticks to them. Consistent expectations across households reduce confusion and help create stability (*see* chapter 14).

Be patient, because it takes time

Trust, respect and love in blended families doesn't happen overnight. Be patient with yourself and with each other. Small progress is still progress, even when it's slow.

Blending families isn't easy, but with the right mindset and support it can lead to strong, loving relationships. The goal isn't to recreate or replace the past – it's to build something new that works for everyone, especially the child.

Tyler's blended birthday celebration

A recent moment of reflection for me came during Tyler's last birthday party. I looked around the room and took in the scene. Tyler's school friends were laughing, his mum's side of the family were chatting, my family were mingling and his stepfather's family was joining in, too. All under one roof.

And right in the middle of it all was Tyler, running around, smiling from ear to ear, completely free – free from tension, from awkward silences, from any sense that the adults in his life were anything but united in their love for him. He moved effortlessly through the room, sharing a laugh with his stepdad, receiving a hug from his grandma, playing with his cousins, without a single hesitation or shadow of worry. And that's exactly how it should be.

That moment reminded me that as adults, especially as co-parents, we have a responsibility to manage ourselves so our children don't have to manage the room. We're the ones who need to leave our egos at the door. We're the ones who must ensure they never feel caught in the middle or forced to choose between love from one side or the other. Because there are no sides. We're all on the same team. And the sooner we realise that, the lighter the load becomes for us, but more importantly, for them. When our children feel safe, loved and supported from every direction, they thrive. That's the real win.

When we work as a team

One of the things that has made life so much smoother, not just for us as adults, but especially for Tyler, is the fact that we've all learned to work together. There have been times when Tyler's mum has had to work late or has been tied up and, instead of it becoming a problem or a point of tension, I've been able to coordinate with his stepfather for pick-ups and drop-offs. On some occasions I've taken Tyler for a haircut and his stepdad has collected him afterwards, saving me the long drive back. Simple things, but they make a big difference.

One day, we even planned a day trip together: just me, Tyler, his stepdad and my eldest son Omari. We spent the afternoon at Gravity in London, racing go-karts, and finished off with Nando's. Tyler absolutely loved it. It was something he asked for, something he genuinely wanted, and yet when I shared it online a few people responded with confusion. One comment stood out: 'There's no need for you to do this.'

But here's the thing: sometimes we do things not because we need to, but because they matter, because they send a message. To our children, these moments say: 'You don't have to choose sides. You're allowed to be loved by everyone in your life, all at once.' That day out wasn't about us as adults. It was about Tyler feeling seen, supported and surrounded by good men who care about him. And what may have looked 'weird' to some, was in fact a gift to him. A memory he still talks about.

Tyler witnessing me and his stepfather interacting positively, laughing, supporting him, enjoying the moment, showed him what respect looks like. What maturity looks like. What putting a child first actually looks like. Remember, these are lessons Tyler will remember not just as a child, but as an adult navigating his own dynamics, however they may look.

Now, I want to pause here and say this: I know this isn't possible for everyone. Some co-parenting dynamics are strained, even unsafe. And if you're in that situation you're not doing anything wrong by setting healthy boundaries. Peace sometimes means separation and your child will still feel your love in other powerful ways. But if you can find an inch of common ground with your co-parent or their new partner, and it's safe to do so, I encourage you to consider the bigger picture. Here are a few benefits for the children when parents and step-parents can work together respectfully:

- **Emotional security:** They don't feel torn between two homes or people they love.
- **Positive role models:** They learn from how you treat one another and it shapes how they approach their own relationships.
- **Consistency and routine:** Communication and cooperation between adults means fewer disruptions for them.
- **A bigger village:** More people cheering them on, guiding them and helping them grow.

So ask yourself:

- Is there a moment where I can extend an olive branch, even in a small way?
- What message do I want my child to internalise about family, respect and relationships?
- Am I acting from love or ego in this situation?

Sometimes what looks 'extra' to others is exactly what your child needs to feel whole. And if we're all on the same team, then showing up, even when it's 'not needed', is part of the job.

#48

Your choices shape their future

Your child, however old they are, is currently the youngest they will ever be. Every single minute, every hour, every day that passes adds to their life and draws them closer to the end of their childhood. Really let that sink in.

And that childhood is not just a fleeting moment; it's the foundation for their future. One day, they will look back on this time and those memories will shape how they view the world, themselves and others. Think about the childhood memories you reflect on with a smile, the ones you wish you could relive, even if just for a moment. With every passing day you have the privilege of helping your child create memories like those.

But there's another side to this. As we grow older, many of us also reflect on the difficult moments from our childhood, the ones that had a lasting impact on who we've become as adults. Maybe it's the unresolved patterns of behaviour you notice in yourself today. Maybe it's the relationships you've struggled with or the emotional baggage you've spent years unpacking. These are often the result of things we saw, heard or experienced when we were young.

Recognising your impact

Now, I'm not saying this to scare you. I'm saying it to wake you up to how important your role is. You're in a powerful position right now. You have the ability to not only shape your child's present, but also their future.

No matter how much we try to protect our children or wrap them in cotton wool, the truth is there will be moments in life that leave a mark; moments we can't predict, prevent or control. Sometimes it might be something they experience at school, a misunderstanding with a friend, or a random event that shakes their world, but the goal isn't to shield them from all trauma, because that's simply not realistic.

Our real goal as parents is to make sure we're not adding unnecessary weight to what life already asks them to carry. It's worth pausing and asking yourself: am I creating a childhood my child will look back on with love or am I unknowingly creating pain that they'll have to heal from later?

Every interaction, every decision and every effort you make in your co-parenting relationship impacts the adult your child will eventually become. You won't get it exactly right – no parent ever does – but if you parent with intention, self-awareness and love, you can tip the balance towards more love, not more hurt.

Parenting with intention means regularly checking in with yourself to ensure the way you show up aligns with the kind of parent you want to be. Even in difficult moments, especially when co-parenting feels challenging or unfair, your ability to lead with intention becomes a model for your child.

You have the choice, right now, to do better for your child. You can decide today to change your outlook, to let go of ego and to be willing to compromise for the sake of their future. This is about what you are willing to do, not about hoping your co-parent will do the same.

Your child's experience, their sense of security and love, will be shaped by what they can consistently expect from you. No matter what your co-parenting relationship looks like, you have the power to create a more peaceful and loving environment for them.

Of course, it would be ideal if your co-parent also chose to meet you in that effort, but their choices are not within your control; your choices are yours, and what you choose will still make a difference.

This isn't about perfection – it's about accountability and awareness. The fact that you're reading this shows that you care and that you are reflecting on what matters most. It's never too late to adjust, to lead by example and to create a healthier dynamic for your child's future.

REFLECTION: PARENTING WITH INTENTION

In parenting, intention starts with you. It's easy to get caught up in what your co-parent is or isn't doing, but the most powerful things you can control are your own behaviour and choices.

- Write down three core values or intentions you want to embody as a parent, for example patience, consistency, kindness or leading by example.
  - How often do your actions reflect these values?
  - Are there moments when you've fallen short?
  - What could you do differently next time?
  - Write down at least three small, consistent steps you can take to live out these intentions more fully.

Keep your self-awareness sharp and remember that the most lasting lessons are taught not by what you say, but by what you consistently do.

A letter to you

Dear parent,

If you've made it this far, I want to thank you, not just for reading, but for choosing to reflect, choosing to pause, choosing to look inwards, even when it's uncomfortable. But before you close this book and return to your daily life, I want to leave you with a reminder: your child is not the aftermath of a broken relationship; they are the purpose you still share.

Your child was created by the two of you. Your child is the living result of two worlds colliding – two families, two stories, two sets of dreams, two completely unique pathways merging into one – and your child needs both of you to thrive and to understand who they are.

This isn't just about fairness or shared responsibilities; it's about identity. Your child isn't just made of skin and bones – they're built from the unseen things, too: inherited mannerisms, generational habits, medical predispositions, family traditions, trauma histories and cultural nuances.

> There is healing and understanding that only you can offer.
>
> There are stories only you can tell.
>
> There are questions only you can answer.

When one parent is absent, emotionally or physically, or intentionally chooses to withhold information, those questions often go unanswered. Questions like:

> Where does my curly hair come from?
>
> Does anyone else in the family struggle with depression?
>
> Why do I feel out of place in both cultures?

Left unanswered, these become emotional potholes in your child's development, places where confusion, self-doubt or resentment can take root. Children start filling in the blanks with their own theories and often those theories are harsh.

As co-parents, it's easy to get wrapped up in logistics, court orders, holidays, pick-ups and drop-offs. The truth is you don't have to be together. You don't even have to like each other. But you do owe your child the dignity of access to their history, their roots and their truth.

Don't let pride or pain make you the reason your child grows up feeling lost and confused in a world that holds no punches. Choose your child over your pride. Every time. Because one day, your child will look back and ask:

Did you do everything you could to put me first?

Did you give me the space to understand all of who I am?

Did you love me enough to put your differences aside for my sake?

When that day comes, let your answer be yes, not just in words, but in the way you showed up. So go forward, not as perfect parents, but as present ones.

Willing to grow. Willing to heal.

Willing to work together.

Willing to build something far stronger than the relationship that broke.

The truth is, I'm still learning, still healing, still becoming, but I know that every time I prioritise joy, growth and self-respect, I'm not just doing it for me. I'm doing it for my children, because a better me always means a better them.

My co-parenting journey has never been easy and as you have learned throughout this book, there have been many bumps, misunderstandings and moments where I have questioned myself, doubted myself as a parent and definitely compared myself to others around me, on social media or within my own family.

But the one thing that has always bought me back to my centre is focusing on my children.

Because everything else is noise; everything else is simply a distraction.

Your child's love is not dependent on parents being together. And they should never be made to feel like it is. And your respect for each other shouldn't vanish just because the intimate relationship is no more.

Be willing to be wrong. Let me say that again: **be willing to be wrong**.

Because when you drop the need to 'win' or be 'right', you create space to grow. And growth is where you become a better person and parent.

One of the biggest barriers I see in co-parenting and in adults generally is stubbornness.

The inability to self-reflect. The refusal to pause and consider another perspective, especially if it challenges how we see ourselves, or, worse, exposes where we may have fallen short.

Your child doesn't need perfect parents. They need accountable ones. They need emotionally safe ones.

Parents who are not afraid to say, 'I got that wrong, and I'm going to do better.'

If you can do that, you break cycles. You change outcomes and give your child a blueprint for relationships, respect, and resilience that will stay with them forever.

References

Should I stay or should I go?

A 2019 Sheffield University study looked at the experiences of over 27,800 households: 'Children's wellbeing not negatively affected by living in single parent households, study shows', Faculty of Social Sciences, University of Sheffield, 8 January 2019. Available at: https://sheffield.ac.uk/social-sciences/news/childrens-wellbeing-not-negatively-affected-living-single-parent-households-study-shows

Why leaving isn't quitting

Direct Line revealed that, on average, parents stay in relationships over five years longer ... And here's the part most people don't talk about: 38% of those children knew ... Even among those parents who stayed, the reasons varied:

'7.6 Million Parents Stay Together Because Of Their Kids', Direct Line Group, 2019. Available at: www.directlinegroup.co.uk/en/news/brand-news/2019/181020190.html

Let's talk about statistics

When we actually look into the stats around single parents: 'Tories have shamed single parents and heaped financial pressure on them' (2022) *The Guardian*. Available at: https://www.theguardian.com/business/2022/jul/05/tories-shamed-single-parents-cost-of-living

In the UK, around 42% of marriages end in divorce: 'Facts and figures about divorce', Harding Evans Solicitors. Available at: www.hardingevans.com/news/2020/10/28/facts-and-figures-about-divorce

... over 2.5 million separated families are currently raising children together: 'Separated families statistics: April 2014 to March 2024', GOV.UK. Available at: www.gov.uk/government/statistics/separated-families-statistics-april-2014-to-march-2024/separated-families-statistics-april-2014-to-march-2024

In the US, the trend is similar, with 40% of children experiencing life with parents: 'Cohabitation and Child Wellbeing', PMC. Available at: https://pmc.ncbi.nlm.nih.gov/articles/PMC4768758/

Dame Rachel de Souza, the Children's Commissioner for England, published a report ... this is backed up by studies that have repeatedly shown that children thrive: 'Independent Family Review', Rachel de Souza, Nuclear Family. Available at: https://assets.childrenscommissioner.gov.uk/wpuploads/2022/12/cc-family-and-its-protective-effect-part-1-of-the-independent-family-review-.pdf

... according to data from Gingerbread, the UK charity that supports single parents ... In the UK, the proportion of single parents who are fathers has remained around 10%: 'Single Parents in 2023', Gingerbread. Available at: www.gingerbread.org.uk/our-work/policy-and-campaigns/research-publications/single-parents-in-2023

In the US, data from the 2024 census: Available at: https://data.census.gov/table?q=ACSDP1Y2024.DP02

Parental involvement in children's early education is consistently found: Hara, S.R. and Burke, D.J., 'Parent involvement: The key to improved student achievement', *The School Community Journal*, 8 (1998), pp. 9–19; Hill, N.E. and Craft, S.A., 'Parent-school involvement and school performance: Mediated pathways among socioeconomically comparable African American and Euro-American families', *Journal of Educational Psychology*, 96 (2003), pp. 74–83; Marcon, R.A., 'Positive relationships between parent school involvement and public school inner-city preschoolers' development and academic performance', *School Psychology Review*, 1999, 28:395–412; Stevenson, D.L. and Baker, D.P. 'The family-school relation and the child's school performance', *Child Development*, 58 (1987), pp. 1348–1357.

Research published in the Journal of Educational Psychology found: Available at: https://www.researchgate.net/publication/232497216_Children%27s_Achievement_in_Early_Elementary_School_Longitudinal_Effects_of_Parental_Involvement_Expectations_and_Quality_of_Assistance

How children view separation

Approximately one in four American children live in a single-parent household: Available at: https://www.census.gov/newsroom/press-releases/2023/children-families-living-arrangements.html

... in Sweden, shared custody is common: Fritzell, S., Gähler, M., Fransson, E., 'Child living arrangements following separation and mental health of parents in Sweden', *SSM Population Health*, 10 (2019).

... highlights that maternal stress is linked to behavioural issues such as anxiety: Available at: https://www.researchgate.net/publication/375712769_Prenatal_stress_and_externalizing_behaviors_in_childhood_and_adolescence_A_systematic_review_and_meta-analysis

Creating two stable homes

... children who experience cooperative co-parenting have better emotional outcomes: Pan, B., *et al.*, 'Parental co-parenting quality, children's emotion regulation abilities, and prosocial behavior', *BMC Psychology*, 13(1) (2025), p. 635.

Parenting plans

Parents who are aligned, and operate from a shared understanding ... Research shows that children benefit directly from this stability ... A large-scale review by Dr Linda Nielsen: Nielsen, L., 'Shared Parenting After Divorce: A Review of Shared Residential Parenting Research', *Journal of Divorce & Remarriage*, 52(8) (2011), pp. 586–609.

School days

... effective parental engagement can lead to learning gains: Education Endowment Foundation. Available at: https://educationendowmentfoundation.org.uk/education-evidence/guidance-reports/supporting-parents

... while a study by an academic called John Hattie: 'Parents Matter: The Research', Parentkind. Available at: www.parentkind.org.uk/for-schools/parents-matter-the-research?utm

Economic abuse

A major study of 540 Australian mothers: Cook, K., Byrt, A., Edwards, T., & Burgin, R., 'Postseparation Financial Abuse Perpetrated Through Government Systems: A Survey of Australian Mothers' Experiences of Child Support', *Violence Against Women*, 3 (2025), pp. 12–13.

A narcissist or just difficult?

... narcissistic personality disorder (NPD) is defined as: American Psychiatric Association, *Diagnostic and statistical manual of mental disorders* (5th ed.) (Washington, DC: American Psychiatric Publishing, 2013)

... individuals with NPD often have troubled relationships: 'Narcissistic personality disorder', Mayo Clinic. Available at: www.mayoclinic.org/diseases-conditions/narcissistic-personality-disorder/symptoms-causes/syc-20366662?

Only around 1% of the population is estimated to have NPD: DeWitt, H., 'Narcissistic tendencies vs. narcissistic personality disorder (NPD): What's the difference?' Thriveworks, 20 June 2025. Available at: https://thriveworks.com/help-with/narcissism/difference-between-npd-and-narcissistic-traits

Alienation effect

In the UK, 200 children lose contact with a parent each day: We Are Fathers4Justice homepage. Available at: www.fathers-4-justice.org

... in the US, studies show that at least 3.9 million children: 'The Devastating Effects of Parental Alienation, Psychology Today, 8 January 2024. Available at: www.psychologytoday.com/gb/blog/head-games/202112/the-devastating-effects-of-parental-alienation

Italian researchers found that individuals who were exposed: Verrochio, M.C., Marchetti, D. and Fulcheri, M. 'Perceived parental functioning, self-esteem, and psychological distress in adults whose parents are separated/divorced', *Frontiers in Psychology*, 6 (2015), p. 1760.

They also found an association between depression in adults: Verrocchio, M.C., Marchetti, D., Carrozzino, D., Compare, A. and Fulcheri, M., 'Depression and quality of life in adults perceived exposure to parental alienation behaviours', *Health and Quality of Life Outcomes*, 17 (2019), pp. 14–23.

In one study, 54% of targeted parents had ideations of suicide ... in another, 24% of study participants had actually attempted it: 'The Effects of PA On The Targeted Parent', The Love and Iron Project. No longer available.

Therapy could be for you

Research shows that parents who understand: Slade, A., (2005). 'Parental reflective functioning: An introduction', *Attachment & Human Development*, 7(3), 269–281. DOI: 10.1080/14616730500245906

Research distinguishes between every day or short-term stress: Shonkoff, J. (2009) 'Investment in Early Child Development lays the foundation for a prosperous and sustainable society', *Encyclopedia on early child development*

As Perry (2002) notes, trauma occurs: Perry, B., (2002) 'Stress, Trauma and Post Traumatic Stress Disorders in children', *Caregiver Education Series, Child Trauma Academy*, Houston TX

... such as poverty, instability or neglect: Walker, *et al* (2011) *Complex PTSD; From surviving to thriving: a guide and map for recovering from childhood trauma*, CreateSpace Independent Publishing Platform Walker, *et al* (2011) 'Inequality in early childhood: risk and protective factors for early child development', *The Lancet*, vol 378, Issue 9799, pp. 1325–38

When to introduce a new partner

... early feelings of love are fuelled by brain regions rich in dopamine and oxytocin: Acevedo, B.P., Poulin, M.J., Collins, N.L. and Brown, L.L., 'After the Honeymoon: Neural and Genetic Correlates of Romantic Love in Newlywed Marriages', *Frontiers in Psychology*, 11 (2020), p. 634.

... this phase can last up to 24 months: Jody Morse, 'How Long Does the Honeymoon Phase Last? What Science Says' Hello, Love, 2024. Available at: https://medium.com/hello-love/how-long-does-the-honeymoon-phase-last-what-science-says-e8d5d80d5fd4

Understanding blended families

... there were over three-quarters of a million stepfamilies:
The majority of step-parents were men ... Around one in 11 children were living in stepfamilies: Children in families in England and Wales: Census 2021, Office for National Statistics. Available at: www.ons.gov.uk/peoplepopulationandcommunity/birthsdeathsandmarriages/families/bulletins/childreninfamiliesinenglandandwales/census2021

Resources

Co-parenting apps
OurFamilyWizard
TalkingParents

Other helpful apps
MindShift CBT – anxiety relief app
Calm – for meditation and sleep

Parenting plan templates
The Children and Family Court Advisory and Support Service (Cafcass) cafcass.gov.uk

Acknowledgements

Co-parenting was never my intention. It was never something I set out hoping for as a parent. It came from relationships not working, from my own immaturity and from having children before I was truly ready to be a father.

But the truth is, this book would not exist without any of that.

This book is me sharing the lessons and experiences I have had to live through, in the hope that you might not have to learn them the same way.

It is a reminder of why our children must always be the focus. A reminder that no matter what we have been through, we still have a choice. A choice to be better and to do better.

Firstly, I want to thank God. Your love, Your consistency, Your never-wavering support has allowed me to create something that I never knew was possible. You heard my prayers when I thought no one was listening, you removed me from places that I would never have left by my own free will, you revealed to me things that I would never have seen, all of which has bought me here today. I am truly grateful for the lessons you have taught me and the ability you placed within me.

To my sons, Omari and Tyler: you have taught me more than I could ever put into words. You have taught me about myself, about my childhood, about fatherhood, and about love. You are a better version of me in the flesh. You are my wrongs turned right.

To the mothers of my children: this journey has not been easy and it is not how any of us imagined things would be. But to see our children happy, settled and thriving is the greatest blessing. You have carried a weight greater than mine and endured more than I ever did. Without you, my children would not be the young men they are today. Thank you for your patience, your effort, and your love for them.

To Aunty Wendy: you have been that rock for me and Mum to lean on over the years and you will never know how much that has meant.

To Abi Fellows: you came into my life at a time when I was being let down by many, and gave me an opportunity I will never forget. More than that, you stayed consistent. Your support has been priceless, and you gave me a lifeline when I needed it most.

To my dad: there was a time when acknowledging you in this book would have been incredibly difficult for me. My ego would have fought against it and the hurt I carried would have made it almost impossible. But writing this book, along with the work I've done on myself over the years, has allowed me to see you through a different lens.

As a man and a father now, not the little boy I once was, I understand that life is a journey of learning, growing and often figuring things out as we go. It's a lesson I've had to learn the hard way myself and one that, at times, affected the mothers of my children. Looking back, I can see that there was once a time when you were simply trying to navigate that same journey too.

This book would not have been possible without the role you have played in my life, whatever shape that role has taken over the years. For that, I am grateful. Thank you for the lessons you have taught me, both directly and indirectly, because many of those lessons have shaped the man I am today, and will now help countless others through the pages of this book.

To my Green Tree and Bloomsbury family, Sarah Skipper, Holly Jarrald, Gloria Amankwaah, Gracia Lukombo, Katherine Macpherson, James Watson and Jason Anscomb: your creativity, care and belief in this project helped turn it into something far beyond what I could have imagined on my own.

To Nieki Shaw, Daniella Kadene and Andrez Harriot: your support, your conversations and your contributions have helped me create something truly special.

To my friends – those who check in daily, weekly or even if months go by, those who have given their time, their ear and their shoulder when I needed it: I see you and I appreciate you. Your messages, your encouragement and your reminders to take care of myself and value myself have meant more than I can ever put into words.

I never wanted to name names, but as a man raised without a father figure, there are a few men who helped shape me into who I am today. Mervyn, Ronnie, Vinton, Maurice, Dwayne: thank you for your guidance and for holding me accountable when I needed it most.

To every single person who has supported my platform, shared a video or commented on a post, even the negative ones: you have all played a part in this book becoming a reality. Your honesty, your vulnerability and your willingness to share your stories have shaped this book more than you know.

And to you, the reader: I pray this book helps you reflect, take responsibility and show up differently for your child, because that's the version of you they deserve.